Dream Yoga

Samael Aun Weor

Dream Yoga
A Glorian Book / 2023

Collected from writings by Samael Aun
Weor, originally published in Spanish.

This Edition © 2023 Glorian Publishing

Print ISBN: 978-1-934206-72-0
Ebook ISBN: 978-1-934206-46-1

Glorian Publishing is a 501(c)3 non-profit organization.
All proceeds go to further the distribution of
these books. For more information, visit glorian.org

Contents

Illustrations

Editor's Introduction

This small collection of writings offers practical guidance from the ancient, universal knowledge of awakening in the internal worlds, otherwise known as dream yoga, lucid dreaming, astral projection, astral travel, or out-of-body experiences (OBEs). The purpose of this book is to empower you with the understanding and skills necessary to acquire your own direct experience of the worlds that exist beyond three-dimensional matter. As such, this is a teaching of Gnosis, a Greek word which refers to knowledge that one acquires through one's own experience, as opposed to knowledge we have heard or been told. "Gnosis" is the name of a timeless and universal teaching that has been present in many times and places around the world, appearing with different names and faces, but always teaching the exact science to awaken the consciousness.

This book offers the essential instructions so that anyone, anywhere, regardless of any distinctions, may enter into their own direct knowledge of the living realities that surround us, yet remain inaccessible to the physical senses.

Although interest in this subject is growing, there are many people who have been frustrated in their attempts to have their own personal experience of the internal worlds. Reading books or attending seminars usually leaves the seeker with more questions, doubts, and contradictions. To those persons, we offer the following quote:

> "We have given many clues in order to consciously travel with the astral body, so thousands of students have learned to travel in their astral body. However, we have seen in practice that those people who cannot quiet the mind, not even for an instant, who are accustomed to hopping from school to school, from lodge to lodge, always inquiring, always preoccupied, are not able to consciously astral travel." —Samael Aun Weor, *The Aquarian Message*

Therefore, understand that this is a scientific, practical, and rigorous effort of working with the consciousness. Information is only useful when it is utilized in the right way. We need Right Effort.

The average person faces two tremendous obstacles when investigating the nature of dreaming and out-of-body experiences: 1) a lack of effective methods, and 2) their own mind.

With this book in hand, you have conquered the first step: here you will find a series of exercises whose potency has been confirmed by thousands of students. These are not mere theories: they are scientific formulae that lead to exact results.

When you put these techniques into activity, the real work begins: to calm your mind. This starts with the awakening of your consciousness here and now, in the physical world, from moment to moment. Without the effort to be consciously awake from moment to moment, dream yoga is impossible. Said another way, the techniques in this book will work for anyone who is making the effort to become consciously awake from moment to moment. But for those who remain dreaming from moment to moment, all day and all night long, these techniques can do nothing. To awaken consciousness, we must stop dreaming, and this must be in each moment.

> "When we are in the physical world, we must learn to be awake from moment to moment. We then live awakened and self-conscious from moment to moment in the internal worlds, both during the hours of the sleep of the physical body and also after death." —Samael Aun Weor, *The Elimination of Satan's Tail*

In other words, if you learn how to awaken your consciousness here and now, then naturally you will awaken consciousness in the internal worlds. In this way, we make steady progress in the elimination of suffering, the understanding of the mysteries of life and death, and the fulfillment of our true reason for being.

Mantra Pronunciation

Chanting or repetition of sacred sounds is universal in all religions. In Sanskrit, these sounds are called mantras, and their repetition is called japa.

Chapter 2

The Awakening of Consciousness

It is necessary to know that humanity lives with its consciousness asleep. People work asleep. People walk through the streets asleep. People live and die asleep.

When we come to the conclusion that the entire world lives asleep, then we comprehend the need to awaken. We need the awakening of the consciousness. We want the awakening of the consciousness.

Fascination

The profound sleep in which humanity lives is caused by fascination.

People are fascinated by everything in life. People forget their Selves because they are fascinated. The drunkard in the bar is fascinated with the alcohol, the place, the pleasures, his friends, and the women. The vain woman in front of a mirror is fascinated with her own glamour. The rich avaricious person is fascinated with money and possessions. The honest worker in the factory is fascinated with the hard work. The father of the family is fascinated with his children. All human beings are fascinated and sleep profoundly. When driving a car we are astonished when we see people dashing across the roads and streets without paying attention to the danger of the running cars. Others willfully throw themselves under the wheels of cars. Poor people... they walk asleep; they look like sleepwalkers. They walk asleep, endangering their own lives. Any clairvoyant can see their dreams. People dream with all that keeps them fascinated.

Sleep

During the physical body's sleep, the ego escapes from it. This departure of the ego is necessary so that the vital body[4] can repair the physical body. However, in the internal worlds we can asseverate that the ego takes its dreams into the internal worlds.

---

4   The subtle, energetic aspect of the physical body, which is in the fourth dimension. It is the body of qi, chi, or vital energy. Related to the sephirah Yesod on the Tree of Life.

Thus, while in the internal worlds the ego occupies itself with the same things which keep it fascinated in the physical world. Therefore, during a sound sleep we see the carpenter in his carpentry shop, the policeman guarding the streets, the barber in his barbershop, the blacksmith at his forge, the drunkard in the tavern or bar, the prostitute in the house of pleasures, absorbed in lust, etc. All these people live in the internal worlds as if they were in the physical world.

During his sleep, not a single living being has the inkling to ask himself whether he is in the physical or astral world.[5] However, those who have asked themselves such a question during sleep, have awoken in the internal worlds. Then, with amazement, they have been able to study all the marvels of the superior worlds.

It is only possible for us to ask such a question of ourselves in the superior worlds (during those hours of sleep) if we accustom ourselves to ask this question from moment to moment during

---

5   The fifth dimension, which is one of the worlds we can experience when we dream. Related to the sephirah Hod on the Tree of Life.

the so-called vigil state. Evidently, during our sleep we repeat everything that we do during the day. Therefore, if during the day we accustom ourselves to asking this question, then, during our nocturnal sleep (while being outside of the body) we will consequently repeat the same question to ourselves. Thus, the outcome will be the awakening of the consciousness.

Remembering Oneself

The human being in its fascinated trance does not remember the Self. We must remember ourselves from moment to moment. We need to remember ourselves in the presence of every representation that could fascinate us. Let us hold ourselves while in front of any representation and ask ourselves: "Where am I? Am I in the physical plane? Am I in the astral plane?" Then, give a little jump with the intention of floating within the surrounding atmosphere. It is logical that if you float it is because you are outside the physical body. Thus, the outcome will be the awakening of consciousness.

The purpose of asking this question at every instant, at every moment is with the intention of engraving it within the subconsciousness, so that it may manifest later during the hours given to sleep, hours when the ego is really outside the physical body. You must know that in the astral plane, things appear just as they are here in this physical plane. This is why during sleep, and after death, people see everything there in a form very similar to this physical world. This is why they do not even suspect that they are outside of their physical body. Therefore, no dead person ever believes himself to have died because he is fascinated and profoundly asleep.

If the dead had made a practice of remembering themselves from moment to moment when they were alive, if they had struggled against the fascination of the things of the world, the outcome would have been the awakening of their consciousness. They would not dream. They would walk in the internal worlds with awakened consciousness. Whosoever awakens the consciousness can study all the marvels of the superior worlds during the hours of sleep. Whosoever awakens the consciousness lives in the superior worlds as a totally awakened citizen of the cosmos. One then coexists with the great hierophants of the White Lodge.[6]

Whosoever awakens the consciousness can no longer dream here in this physical plane or in the internal worlds. Whosoever awakens the consciousness stops dreaming. Whosoever awakens the consciousness becomes a competent investigator of the superior worlds. Whosoever awakens consciousness is an illuminated one. Whosoever awakens the consciousness can study at the feet of the master. Whosoever awakens the consciousness can talk familiarly with the gods who initiated the dawn of creation. Whosoever awakens the consciousness can remember his innumerable reincarnations. Whosoever awakens the consciousness can consciously attend his own cosmic initiations. Whosoever awakens the consciousness can study in the temples of the great White Lodge. Whosoever

6   The ancient collection of pure souls who maintain the highest and most sacred of sciences: White Magic or White Tantra. It is called "white" due to its purity and cleanliness (ie. no ego, lust, pride, attachment, etc). This "Brotherhood" or "Lodge" includes human beings of the highest order from every race, culture, creed and religion, and of both sexes.

awakens the consciousness can know
in the superior worlds the evolution of
his Kundalini.[7] Every perfect matrimony
must awaken the consciousness in order
to receive guidance and direction from
the White Lodge. In the superior worlds
the masters will wisely guide all those who
really love one another. In the superior
worlds the masters give to each one that
which one needs for inner development.

Complementary Practice

Every Gnostic student, after waking
from their normal sleep, must perform a
retrospective exercise based on the process
of their sleep, in order to remember all of
those places they visited during the hours
of sleep. We already know that the ego
travels a great deal; it goes towards where
we have physically been, repeating all that
which we have seen and heard.

The masters instruct their disciples
when they are out of the physical body.

Therefore, it is urgent to know how
to profoundly meditate and then practice
what we have learned during the hours

---

7   The divine fire that awakens in the devotee who
     earns it; see glossary.

of sleep. It is necessary not to physically move at the time of waking up, because with the movement, the astral body is agitated and the memories are lost. It is urgent to combine the retrospective exercises with the following mantras:

RAOM GAOM[8]

Each word is divided into two syllables. One must accentuate the vowel **O**. These mantras are for the student what dynamite is for the miner. Thus, as the miner opens his way through the bowels of the earth with the aid of dynamite, similarly, the student also opens his way into the memories of his subconsciousness with the aid of these mantras.

Patience and Tenacity

The Gnostic student must be infinitely patient and tenacious because powers cost a great deal. Nothing is given to us for free. Everything has a price. These studies are not for inconsistent people, nor for people of fragile will. These studies demand infinite faith.

---

8   Pronounced as Latin: A: as the ah in "father." O: as the oh in "holy." M: extended as if humming, "mmmmm. G: pronounced as in "give."

Skeptical people must not come to our studies because esoteric science is very demanding. The skeptics fail totally. Thus, skeptical people will not succeed in entering the Heavenly Jerusalem.

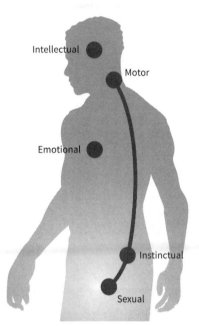

THREE BRAINS / FIVE CENTERS

Chapter 3
On Dreams

Gnosis teaches that the modern, decadent psychology of the western hemisphere is ignorant of the various kinds of dreams that exist.

Dreams have a diverse and specific quality, for they are closely related to each of the psychic centers of the human body. In fact, we do not exaggerate when we state that most dreams are linked to the motor-instinctual center. That is, they are the echoes of everything we see during the day: simple sensations and motions—a mere astral repetition of our daily life.

Some emotional experiences, such as fear—which harms humanity so much— usually fit in those chaotic dreams of the motor-instinctive centers as well.

There are, then, emotional, sexual, intellectual, motor, and instinctual dreams.

The more important dreams, the inner experiences of the Being,[9] are asso-

---

9   Our inner, divine source, also called the Inner-most or Monad, which is not easily definable in conceptual terms. See glossary for more.

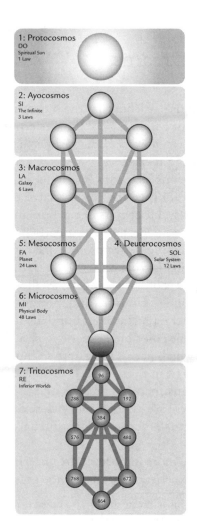

THE DESCENT OF THE RAY OF CREATION ALONG THE TREE OF LIFE (KABBALAH)

ciated with the two centers: the superior emotional and the superior intellectual.

Dreams related to the superior centers are certainly interesting. Their main feature is what we could call a "dramatic array."

Now then, if we think of the Ray of Creation,[10] the superior and inferior centers, and the influences descending through the cited cosmic ray, we must admit that some luminous vibrations appear. These intend to heal us, to inform us about the state in which we are, and more.

It is useful to receive messages and to be in contact with the Aztec, Mayan, Toltec, Egyptian, and Greek adepts.

It is marvelous, as well, to have intimate dialogue with the highest, diverse parts of our Being.

The superior centers are fully developed in us, and they send us messages which we must learn to consciously grasp.

---

10 The light of the Ain Soph Aur, also known as the Okidanokh, Quetzalcoatl, Kulkulcan, Krestos, and Christ. This ray descends like a lightning bolt, creating and illuminating all the levels of existence.

In this chapter, those select people who have had a moment of Self-remembrance[11] (in which they saw a common thing or person in a totally different way) will not be surprised if I tell them that such moments have the same quality as one of those rare and strange dreams related to the two superior centers (emotional and intellectual). The meaning of such transcendental dreams matches, undoubtedly, the same level of realization in oneself of the Ray of Creation, and, in particular, the lateral octave of the Sun. The beginning of our realization of the deep significance of this specific type of dream is the signal that some forces struggle to awaken, heal, or cure us.

Each of us is a mathematical point in space that is used as a vehicle by determined sums of "values" (black or white).

Death is a subtraction of fractions. Once the mathematical operation is complete, the only thing left are the "values" (good or bad).

---

11 A state of active consciousness, controlled by will, that begins with awareness of being here and now. See glossary for more information.

In accordance with the law of eternal return,[12] it is certain that the "values" return; they are re-embodied.

If a man starts taking into account more consciously the small cycle of recurring events of his personal life, he will be able to verify directly, through mystical experience, that in daily sleep the same mathematical operation of death is always repeated.

In the absence of the physical body during normal sleep, the "values" merge into the Astral Light[13] and attract or repel each other in accordance with the law of universal magnetization.

The return to the vigil state rightfully implies the return of the "values" to the interior of the physical body.

Extraordinarily, people think that they only interrelate with the external world.

---

12 The process of the soul entering into a new born physical body as determined by karma and circumstance, rather than "by choice" as is popularly imagined. See glossary.

13 "There is one vital substance in Nature upon which all things subsist. It is called archæus, or vital life force, and is synonymous with the astral light or spiritual air of the ancients." — Manly P. Hall

Gnosis teaches us that we interrelate with an inner world, which is invisible to the physical, ordinary senses, but visible to clairvoyance.[14]

This inner, invisible world is much wider, and it contains many more interesting things than the external world where the five windows of the senses are always opened.

Many dreams relate to the place where we are in the inner, invisible world from which the diverse circumstances of life come forth.

The language of dreams is accurately comparable to the language of parables.

Those who interpret everything literally, think that the sower of the Christic Gospel went to sow, and that the seeds fell on rocks, and so on, but they do not understand the sense of the parable, because it belongs to the symbolic language of the superior emotional center.

Needless to say here that any dream, as absurd or incoherent as it may be, has some significance for it indicates not only the psychic center to which it is associated

---

14 "Clear seeing." The power of imagination developed to a degree that it can perceive other dimensions, such as the worlds of emotions, thoughts, causes, etc.

but also the psychological status of such a center.

Many penitent people, who presumed to be chaste, failed in the sexual center, and had a nocturnal pollution when they were submitted to trials in the internal world.

In the perfect adept, the five psychic centers—intellectual, emotional, motor, instinctive, and sexual—function in full harmony with the infinite...

What is our mental activity during sleep? What emotions move or shatter us? What are our activities outside the physical body? What instinctive sensations predominate? Have we considered our sexual states during sleep?

We must be sincere with ourselves. Plato rightfully said, "A man is known by his dreams."

The matter of the erroneous work of the centers is a topic that demands a lifetime of study by way of the observation of oneself in action and of the rigorous examination of dreams.

It is not possible to achieve the understanding of the centers and their correct or incorrect function in an instant. We need infinite patience.

All of life unfolds as a function of the centers and is controlled by them.

Our thoughts, ideas, feelings, hopes, fears, love, hatred, deeds, sensations, pleasure, satisfactions, frustrations, and so on are found in the centers.

The discovery of some inhuman element in any of the centers must be the strongest motive for the esoteric work.

Any psychological defect must be previously understood by way of the technique of meditation before proceeding to its elimination.

The extirpation, eradication, or elimination of any undesirable element is only possible by invoking Tonantzin's aid (our Divine Mother Kundalini),[15] a variation of our own Being, or particular Fohat of each of us.

This is how we die from moment to moment. Only death brings forth what is new.

Influences of all kinds reach us in the levels of beings and things. If we have understood the Ray of Creation, we will also acknowledge that, in any instant of life, influences, which are of various qualities, reach us.

---

15 See glossary.

We must always be aware that there are superior influences that act upon us and are recorded by our psychic system. If we are, nevertheless, attached to our senses, and we do not pay full attention to our inner life, we will not be able to perceive these influences.

JACOB'S VISION

"When the mind is quiet and silent — free
of daily routine and mundane anxiety — it is
then in a state that is one hundred percent
favorable for the Dream Yoga practice."

Chapter 4

Dreams and Visions

Gnostic students must learn to differentiate between dreams and visions. To dream is one thing and to have visions, another. A truly "awakened" Gnostic cannot dream. Only those who have the consciousness asleep live dreaming.

The worst type of dreamer is the sexual dreamer. Those who live dreaming of carnal passions stupidly waste their creative energy in the satisfaction of their fantastic pleasures. Ordinarily, these people do not progress in their business. They fail in every sense. They end up in misery.

When we look at a pornographic image, it strikes the senses and then passes to the mind. The psychological "I" intervenes in these affairs by stealing the erotic image in order to reproduce it in the mental plane. Thus, in the world of the mind, that image is transformed into a living effigy [a succubus or incubus].[16] During sleep, the dreamer fornicates[17]

16 See glossary: elementaries.
17 See glossary: fornication.

with that living effigy, which like an erotic demon tempts the dreamer for the satisfaction of the lust. The outcome is wet dreams with all their horrible consequences. Therefore, the true devotees of the path must not visit cinemas because they are dens of black magic. The erotic figures of the screen give rise to mental effigies and erotic dreams. In addition, the cinemas are full of diabolic elementaries[18] created by the human mind. Those malignant elementaries damage the mind of the spectators.

The subconscious mind creates fantastic dreams within the realm of dreams. The quality of dreams depends on the beliefs of the dreamer. When someone believes we are good, he dreams about us, seeing us as angels. When someone believes we are bad, he dreams about us, seeing us in the form of a devil.

Many things come into our memory whilst writing these lines. In the past when we, the brothers and sisters, worked in various countries, we were able to observe that whilst our Gnostic disciples believed in us, they dreamed seeing us as angels. It was sufficient for them to stop

18   See glossary.

believing in us for them to then dream about us being demons. Those who swore before the altar to follow and obey us, admired us with great enthusiasm and dreamed seeing us as being angels. Many times it was enough for those students to have read a book or to have listened to some lecturer in order for them to become affiliated with a new school. Then, having stopped believing in us, having changed their concept and opinions, they dreamed about us, seeing us changed into devils. Then, which clairvoyance do these people possess? What became of their clairvoyant dreams? What type of clairvoyant today sees us as gods and tomorrow affirms that we are devils? Where is the clairvoyance of these dreamers? Why do these people contradict themselves? Why do they swear today that we are gods and tomorrow swear that we are devils? What is this?

The subconsciousness is a screen upon which many internal films are projected.

Nowadays, the subconsciousness sometimes acts as a cameraman, other times as a director, and also as a projectionist who projects images onto the mental background.

It is clear that our subconscious projector usually commits many errors. No one ignores that erroneous thoughts, groundless suspicions, and also false dreams emerge on the screen of the mind.

We need to transform the subconsciousness into consciousness, to stop dreaming, to awaken the consciousness.

Whosoever awakens is incapable of dreaming. Thus, while his physical body sleeps within the bed, he lives in a state of intensified vigilance within the internal worlds. Such people are authentic illuminated seers.

We frankly cannot accept clairvoyants who have not awakened their consciousness. We cannot accept clairvoyants who have not engendered the Christ-astral, Christ-mind, and Christ-will.[19] Those clairvoyants who have neither awakened consciousness nor possess their Christic vehicles can only see their own beliefs and concepts in the internal worlds. In short, they are useless.

19 These are, respectively, the solar astral body (Hod), solar mental body (Netzach), and solar causal body (Tiphereth), each of which is created through sexual transmutation and degrees of internal initiation. Read *The Perfect Matrimony* by Samael Aun Weor.

Only those awakened clairvoyants, only those clairvoyants who already possess their Christic vehicles are worthy of true credit. They are not dreamers. They do not make mistakes. They are true illuminates. Such people are in fact true masters of the White Lodge. The visions of this class of sublime humans are not simple dreams. These are the Masters of Perfection. This kind of master cannot dream any more. This class of master can investigate the memories of Nature and read in the sealed archives of creation all the history of the Earth and its races.

Everyone who follows the path of the perfect matrimony should live alert and vigilant as a watchman in the time of war, because during the hours of sleep the masters test their disciples. Yet, the tenebrous ones attack us during sleep when we are working in the Great Work. Thus, during sleep, we have to pass through many ordeals in the internal worlds.

When the masters are going to test the disciple in something, then they awaken the disciple's consciousness.

THE DIVINE MOTHER AS DEPICTED BY THE GREEKS WITH THE TWO
SYMBOLIC SERPENTS: ONE POSITIVE UNDER HER HAND (THE HINDU
KUNDALINI, AND THE SERPENT OF MOSES) AND THE NEGATIVE
SERPENT, REPRESENTED BY THE HEAD OF MEDUSA ON HER CHEST.

Chapter 5

Key of SOL

Unquestionably, the most important thing in life is the realization of the inner Being.

Once, I interrogated my Divine Mother Kundalini, as follows: "How is it that the path that leads to the resurrection[20] is extremely long?"

She answered me, "It is not that the path is too long; rather, the work with the philosophical stone is very hard: it must be worked, chiseled. It is necessary to give the brute stone a perfectly cubic shape."

Our motto is Thelema, meaning "willpower."

We must begin by awakening the consciousness. Obviously, all human beings are asleep, and in order to see the path it is necessary to be awakened; thus, what is essential is to awaken here and now.

---

20 Resurrection occurs on the Direct Path at the end of the Second Mountain, after the elimination of all of the ego and karma, thus like Jesus one emerges from the grave anew, perfect. Read *The Three Mountains* by Samael Aun Weor.

Unfortunately, people sleep; it seems incredible, but this is how it is.

We wander in the streets with the consciousness asleep; we are in our house, in our job, in the body shop, in the office, etc., with the consciousness profoundly asleep. We drive our car and we go to the factory with the consciousness tremendously asleep.

People are born, they grow, they breed, they get old and die with the consciousness asleep; thus, they never know where they come from nor the objective of their existence. What is most grave in this matter is that all of them believe that they are awake.

For instance, many people are preoccupied in knowing many esoteric things, yet they never occupy themselves with the awakening of their consciousness. If people had the purpose of awakening here and now, then immediately they could know all of that which for them are enigmas; this is why skepticism exists, because the skeptical is ignorant, and ignorance is the outcome of a sleeping consciousness. Indeed, I want to tell you in the name of the truth that skepticism exists because of ignorance. Therefore, the day when the people awaken their consciousness they will stop being ignorant, and, as a fact, skepticism will disappear, because ignorance is equal to skepticism and vice versa.

Indeed, Gnosis is not a doctrine that seeks to convince skeptical people, because if today we convince 100 skeptical individuals, tomorrow we have to convince 10,000, and if we convince the 10,000, then 100,000 will appear who want to be convinced, and so on and so forth; thus, we will never be done.

The system to attain the inner realization of the Being is a matter of cognizant works and voluntary sufferings, yet continuity of purpose in the three factors[21] of the revolution of the consciousness is necessary. Logically, in order to achieve the awakening of the consciousness, it is necessary to die from instant to instant, from moment to moment.

---

21 The three factors are:
1. To be born as a soul; the liberation and actualization of virtues
2. To die psychologically; mystical death; the decapitation of the ego; purification of pride, anger, lust, envy, etc.
3. To sacrifice for others; service, charity, self-lessness, altruism, bodhichitta, etc.

The sleeping person ends up intoxicated when in the presence of a cup of liquor. The sleeping person ends up fornicating when in the presence of the opposite sex. Thus, the sleepy ones becomes identified with everything that surrounds them, and forget themselves.

From my memory—at this very moment—I recall the unusual case of Piotr Demianovich Ouspensky, who when walking on the streets of Saint Petersburg, had the resolve to remember himself, and to not forget about himself, not even for an instant. Thus, he said that as he remembered himself from moment to moment, he even perceived a spiritual aspect within all things, and while this type of spiritual lucidity was increasing he felt his psyche gradually transformed, etc. Nevertheless, something very discouraging happened to him: all of a sudden he felt the necessity to enter a smoke shop in order to select an order of some tobacco. Certainly, after being attended and provided with his order of cigars, he left the smoke shop very quietly while smoking along an avenue. Thereafter, remembering different things and occupied in diverse intellectual matters, etc., he walked through different places of Saint Petersburg; in other words, he became absorbed within his thoughts.

An hour and a half later—already at his home—he observed very well his room, his bedroom, his living room, his desk, etc., and suddenly, he remembered that he had first wandered through many places with his consciousness awake, but after having entered into the cigarette shop his psyche had fallen asleep again, and thus, his good intentions of remaining awake from moment to moment were reduced to cosmic dust; thus, he regretted the incident. He took an hour and a half to reach his home, and during that entire time, he regrettably walked the streets of the city with his consciousness completely asleep.

Behold how difficult it is to remain with the consciousness awake from instant to instant, from moment to moment, from second after second. However, if one has true longings for becoming fully awakened—this is the beginning—one must not forget oneself, not even for a moment.

Yes, one must keep remembering oneself wherever one walks—in any living room, or on whichever street one goes by

walking, jogging, or riding a car, whether
it be night or day—wherever one might
be, at work or in the shop, anywhere:
one must remember oneself while at the
presence of any beautiful object, or while
before any window-shop where very beautiful things are being shown, etc.—in other
words, one must not become identified
with anything that one likes or is captivated by.

Subject

The person needs to always keep
remembering himself: not only his physicality, but also one needs to watch one's
own thoughts, feeling, emotions, deduc-
tions, desires, fears, longings, etc.

Object

Beloved brothers and sisters, it seems
to me that this second aspect (object)
is abundantly intriguing, because it is
related with becoming inquisitive about
objects, that is, with "not becoming identified with things" as we already stated;
thus, if you see a beautiful object—i.e. a
suit within a window-store, or an expo-

sition of something, or an exhibition of anything: a very beautiful car, a pair of wonderful shoes, anything—what is important is to not become identified with the thing, and to know how to distinguish between common things and uncommon things, like a strange animal, an elephant that flies, or a camel that appears in the middle of the living-room, etc.; thus, the first thing that one needs to do is to reflect.

One needs to not become identified with the object or creature that one sees, because if one becomes identified with what one sees, that is, if one is absorbed by the representation before one's eyes, then one remains fascinated; in other words, one passes from identification to fascination, and this is how one remains enchanted, marveled, identified. If one forgets oneself, then thereafter one's own consciousness falls asleep; it will snooze profoundly.

Thus, my dear brothers and sisters, the only thing that one achieves with this mistaken behavior—that is, by allowing oneself to become foolishly fascinated with objects—is to deactivate the consciousness, to put it to sleep, and this is critical, very critical, very critical... very critical...

Location

From my memory—at his very moment—I recall another unusual case: many years ago when I was traveling through the countries of South America—since as a traveler I always walked from one country to another around the world—on a given night it so happened that I saw myself walking through a garden, then into a living room and through it, and finally I arrived at a lawyer's office, where I saw seated at a desk a lady of a certain age, with grey hair, who very amiably attended me; she stood up and greeted me.

Suddenly, I observed that two butterflies made of crystal were on the desk—well, there is nothing odd about seeing two butterflies on a desk, right? Yet, the intriguing aspect of this matter is that the two butterflies were alive: they were moving their wings, their little heads, their little legs, and that is very odd, right? So, this was very unusual and intriguing: two butterflies made of crystal, and alive! These butterflies were not normal; it is clear that they were not natural, my beloved brothers and sisters, this was something odd; it was a case where one has to become very inquisitive.

Well then, do you want to know what I did? I did not become identified with the pair of butterflies, I only pondered the following question within myself: "How is it possible that there exist in the world butterflies whose bodies are made of crystal, whose head, legs, and wings are made of crystal, and that breathe and have life like the natural ones?" Thus, this is how I reflected, my beloved brothers and sisters.

What if I had become identified with the butterflies and not pondered an analytical question, without reflecting on those butterflies made of crystal? What if I had become fascinated, or enchanted, and had fallen into unconsciousness? Well, that would have been foolish, right?

However, I reflected, by pondering the following statements to myself: "No! It is impossible for these type of creatures to exist in the physical world. No, no, no, this is very strange, this is very odd, this is not normal. Here, I smell something fishy; there is something rare. This type of phenomenon, as I know, does not exist in the tridimensional world, since this is only possible in the astral world; it seems that I am in the astral dimension; could it be that I am in the astral world?"

Then, I question myself: "It seems that I am dreaming, it seems that I left my physical body sleeping somewhere, because indeed this is very odd. So, in order to be sure, I am going to perform a small jump with the intention of floating in the environment; thus, this is how I will verify if I am in my astral body, so let us see what happens." So, this is what I said to myself; yes brothers and sisters, with complete confidence I tell you that this is how I proceeded. It is obvious that I had to proceed in that manner and not in another manner, right? However, I was concerned about jumping in front of that lady; thus, I said to myself, "This lady might think that I am a nut case if I start jumping here in her office."

Apparently, everything was very normal: a desk like any desk, the chair where the lady was seated was one of those that rotate from one side to the other. There were two candelabra in that office; I remember that one was at the right and the other at the left; they seem made of massive gold. So, I remember this with entire exactitude, my dear brothers and sisters, even though it happened a long time ago, many years, since I was very young in that epoch. Thus, I remember that the candelabra had seven branches. Well, talking here with complete confidence, I did not find anything odd in that room, everything was normal in that office; however, when I focused my sight in those butterflies they became the only truly questionable oddity there. As for the rest, I said: "There is nothing odd about this lady, she as normal as other ladies in the world; however, these butterflies make me intrigued." The fact that they were alive on their own accord was very rare. Anyhow, be that as it may, I resolved to leave the room with the intention of performing a little jump, do you understand? Of course, I had to give an excuse to the lady, thus, I asked her consent to leave the office; I told her that I needed to leave the room just for a moment, and that I did.

Thus, when outside in the corridor and being sure that no one was looking at me, I performed a long jump with the intention of floating in the environment...

and behold, let me tell you what happened, sincerely I tell you that I immediately remained floating in the surrounding atmosphere. Of course, I felt a delectable sensation, my dear brothers and sisters, a delectable sensation; then I said to myself: "I am in my astral body; here I do not have even the slightest doubt about it." I remembered that a few hours before I had left my physical body sleeping in my bed and by displacing myself there in the astral world I had arrived to that place, to that office.

Then, I went back into that office, I sat again before the lady and spoke to her with much respect. I told her, "Be aware, ma'am, that we both are in the astral body." Wondering, with sleepy eyes as a somnambulist, that lady scarcely looked at me; she did not understand, she did not comprehend, nevertheless, I wanted to clarify the situation for her and I told her, "Ma'am, remember that a few hours ago you went to bed, to lay down in order to sleep, therefore, do not wonder why am I telling you this; listen: your physical body is sleeping in your bed and you are here talking with me in the astral world..."

Yet, definitively, that lady did not understand; she was profoundly asleep, she had her consciousness asleep. Thus, upon seeing that everything was useless, comprehending that she would not awaken—not even with cannon shots, since that wretched lady had never dedicated herself to the labor of the awakening of her consciousness—then frankly, my dear brothers and sisters, I resolved to apologize, and left.

Well, as a curious thing, I want to narrate for you that many years after, maybe 30 years or more, I had to travel to Taxco, Guerrero, Mexico. Taxco is a very beautiful town, situated over a hill and built in the colonial style; its streets are stone-paved as in the epoch of the colonization, and it is very rich indeed; it has many silver mines, and many beautiful objects and jewelry made of silver are sold there.

I had to travel to that town because someone I was making some remedies for lived there; he wanted to be healed and wanted me to help him in his healing process; he was a wretched patient, very sick...

Well, I arrived at a house, I crossed a garden, and arrived at the living room, which I recognized immediately. There was a lady; I looked at her and recognized her: she was the same lady that I had seen behind the desk many years ago in the astral world; however, this time she was in the living room.

She invited me to pass into another room, where I found the already mentioned lawyer's office, where I, so many years ago, had arrived in my astral body. Yet now, instead of the lady behind the desk, it was her husband, a very well educated man who without a title was dedicated to the law (in some places these people are called interns); well, call them as you please. The fact was that he was seated there, in that office. He stood in order to welcome me and thereafter he invited me to sit down in front of his desk. So, I had immediately recognized the office and the lady.

Then, it so happened that because that man liked a little these sort of spiritual studies, we talked and conversed for a while on these matters; he liked everything related with esoteric studies. Thus, I surprised him a little when I told him, "Sir, I was here already some time ago. I was out of my physical body, in my astral body, and you know that one moves, walks, and goes from one place to another." This gentleman already knew a little about these things, so my statement was not unusual to him.

Then I told him, "See, on this desk there were two butterflies made of crystal. What happened, where are those butterflies?"

He quickly answered me, "Here are the butterflies, right here, look at them." He then raised some newspapers that were upon the desk and certainly, they were there, the two very beautiful butterflies made of crystal... Of course, he was very astounded that I knew about those butterflies.

Then I told him, "But something else is missing. I see one candelabra of seven arms, yet I saw two. Where is the other, what happened to it?"

"Here is the other one, look at it," the gentleman in his office answered me. He then removed some papers and newspapers that he had there and indeed he showed me the other candelabra; yes, it appeared in order to confirm my assertions even more. Of course, the man was amazed.

Then I told him, "I want you to know that I know your wife, because when I came here your wife was at the desk." Well, the gentleman was amazed.

Thus, at dinner time we were seated at a round table and something truly unexpected happened: in the presence of her husband, the lady told me, "I met you a long time ago. I do not know exactly where, but I have seen you... Yes, I have seen you before in some place. Anyhow, you are not an unknown person to me."

Then, I immediately elbowed the gentleman and told him, "Do you realize it? Are you convinced of my words?"

Well, the amazement of that man reached its maximum. Unfortunately— and this indeed is what is very critical, my beloved brothers and sisters—that man was so attached to his sect, which we might call a type of Roman sect, that frankly speaking, he did not enter into the path due to sectarian matters. Otherwise, he would have come to the path, because I gave him extraordinary evidence that for him was factual and definite; at least, he became forever amazed, did he not? Regrettably, his beliefs did not allow him, they confused him; he became entangled

in all those religious dogmas, etc. Well,
many years have already passed, nevertheless I have been able to narrate this event
for you.

Thus, this is why I recommend to you
the division of attention into three parts:

1. Subject

That is to say: oneself. One must not
forget oneself, not even for an instant.

2. Object

Observe all things, as in the case of
the butterflies that I have narrated to you.
What if in this very moment in which
you are reading this book, a person that
died many years ago arrived to your home
and spoke to you. Would you be so naive,
would you be so absent minded, as to not
ask yourself, "What is this? Could it be
that I am in my astral body?" Would you
be as reckless as to not do the experiment
and to give a little jump? Well then, do
not forget that any detail, as insignificant
as it may appear, must be enough in order
to perform this type of inquisition. Thus,
every object must be studied in detail, and

thereafter one must ask oneself, "Why am I here?"

3. Place

One must not live unconsciously. When we arrive at any place, we must observe it in detail, very minutely, and thereafter ask ourselves, "Why am I here, in this place?" And by the way, you that are reading this book, tell me: did you already ask yourself why you are there in that place where you are reading? Did you already inconvenience yourself to observe that place, the ceiling or the walls, or the space that surrounds you? Are you already observing the floor or the place, up and down, to the sides, behind you, and in front of you? Did you already look at the walls and your surroundings in order to ask the question, "Where am I?" And if you did not do it, why do not you try? Or, perhaps you are reading this book unconsciously?

It is clear that you must never live unconsciously, no matter where you are: in a house, on the street, in a temple, or in a taxi, on the sea, or in an airplane, etc. So, wherever you may be, wherever you are to be found, the first thing that you must ask yourself is, "Why am I in this place?"

Look minutely at everything that surrounds you: the ceiling, the walls, the floor; that observation is not only for the park, the house, or an unknown place, but one must do it daily, all the time. Look at your house as if it was something new or unknown; do so every time and every moment that you enter into it. You must also ask yourself, "Why am I in this house? What a strange house..." Then look at the ceiling, the walls, and the ground, at the patio, etc.—everything in detail—then ask yourself the question, "Why am I in this place? Could it be that I am in my astral body?" Thereafter, perform a little extended jump with the intention of floating in the environment.

If you do not float, but still feel that you are in your astral body, then go stand on top of a chair or on of a low table, an ottoman, a strong box, or something of the sort, and jump in the air with the intention of floating. Sometimes one performs the extended jump and nevertheless one does not float. Thus, the best solution is to go and stand on something that allows us to jump in the air in order to hover in the environment when one jumps with the intention of flying. Thus, it is clear that if one is in the astral world, one remains floating in the environment, and if not, then one returns to the ground.

So, do not forget the division of attention into three parts:

Subject

Object

Location

If one becomes accustomed to live with the attention divided into these three parts—subject, object, and location—if one is habituated to do it daily, at every moment, from instant to instant, from second to second, then this habit becomes recorded deeply in the consciousness; thus, at night, when our physical body sleeps, one performs the exercise in the astral world, one does the same thing that one does in the physical body: the outcome is the awakening of the consciousness.

You know that often at night you repeat in dreams the same things that you usually do during the day. For example, during the day many work in a factory, or as traveling salesmen, or in an office, then at night during their dreams they see themselves working, doing exactly the same things that they do during the day: they dream that they are in the factory, or selling, or in the office, etc. It is clear that everything that you do during the day you repeat during the night, that is to say, you dream the same thing at night.

So, it is a matter of performing this practice during the day, at every hour, at every moment or second, in order to achieve it during the night, and thus awaken our consciousness.

It is clear that when any person is physically sleeping, the Essence, the consciousness, is far from the physical body; then it so happens that when the Essence is outside of the physical body, it acts within the astral body, and repeats the same things that it does during the day. This is how you can awaken automatically, because the practice of this exercise gives a spark or shock to your consciousness, which then remains awake.

Thus, my dear brothers and sisters, when one is already awake in the astral world, one can invoke the masters, for example, one can call the Angel Anael or the Angel Adonai—the child of light and happiness—or the Master Khut Humi, so that they can come to instruct us, to teach us, etc. Likewise, you can call any other Master, namely Morya, the Count Saint Germain, etc. and those who invoke me they can be sure that I will concur to their call; they should be sure.

Therefore, I give you the system in order to receive the teachings directly, and if you want to remember your past lives, then invoke the masters of the White Lodge, Khut Humi, Hilarion, Morya, etc., and ask them to have the amiability, the kindness, to help you to remember your former existences, to help you to recall your past lives. You can be sure that the masters will grant you such a petition.

This system that I am giving to you all is in order for you to receive the direct knowledge. You can also travel to Eastern Tibet, you can also go to the depth of the oceans, including to other planets if you want...

Thus, this is the way to receive direct knowledge. This is why I tell you:

Awaken, my dear brothers and sisters. Awaken. Awaken. Do not continue living your life as unconscious or asleep individuals, as this is very sad, my dear brothers and sisters.

Behold the sleepy souls, how they walk unconsciously in the astral world, and after death they continue asleep, unconscious, and dreaming foolishness. They are born without knowing at what time. They die without knowing at what time. I do not want that you continue like this, within that terrible unconsciousness. I want you to awaken.

"Alas, now as the intermediate state of dreams arises before me, renouncing the corpse-like, insensitive sleep of delusion, I must enter, free from distracting memories, the state of the abiding nature of reality. Cultivating the experience of inner radiance, through the recognition, emanation, and transformation of dreams, I must not sleep like a beast, but cherish the experiential cultivation which mingles sleep with actual realization."

—Padmasambhava, Root Verses of the Six Intermediate States

Chapter 6

Dream Yoga Discipline

Those candidates who sincerely long for a mystical, direct experience must unquestionably begin with the dream yoga[22] discipline.

The Gnostic must be very demanding with himself and learn to create favorable conditions to remember and understand all those inner experiences that always occur during sleep.

Before retiring to our bed at the end of our daily routine, it is advisable to pay attention to the state we are in.

Devotees whose circumstances make them lead a sedentary life will gain a lot if before going to bed they have a short but very lively walk outdoors. A walk will relax the muscles. I must clarify, however, that we must never abuse physical exercises; we need to live in harmony.

Supper or the final meal of the day must be light and free of heavy or stimu-

---

22 (Tibetan rmi-lam) The science of awakening consciousness in the dream state, transforming it into an opportunity for spiritual development.

lating foods. Foods that keep us awake or alter our sleep should be avoided.

The highest way of thinking is not thinking. When the mind is quiet and silent—free of daily routine and mundane anxiety—it is then in a state that is one hundred percent favorable for the dream yoga practice. When the superior emotional center is actually working, the thinking process stops, at least for a brief moment. Clearly, that is activated with Dionysian intoxication. Such rapture is possible when listening with infinite devotion to the delightful symphonies of Wagner, Mozart, Chopin, and others. Beethoven's music is especially extraordinary because it makes the superior emotional center vibrate intensely. The sincere Gnostic finds in it a vast field for mystical exploration, for it is not music of form, but of archetypal, ineffable ideas. Every note has a meaning; every pause is a superior emotion.

Beethoven, when feeling the cruel rigors and trials of the "spiritual night," instead of failing, as many candidates did, opened the eyes of his intuition to the mysterious supernatural, the spiritual side of Nature, to that region where angelic kings of these universal creations (Tlaloc, Ehecatl, Huehueteotl, etc.) live.

Observe the musician-philosopher all along his exemplary existence. On top of his working desk, he always had in plain view his Divine Mother Kundalini, the ineffable Neith, Anahuac's Tonantzin, the supreme Egyptian Isis. It has been said that the cited great master had an inscription at the base of that adorable sculpture, written with his own hand, that mysteriously asserted: "I am she who has been, is and will be; no mortal has lifted my veil."

Revolutionary and inner progress is impossible without the immediate aid of our Divine Mother Tonantzin.

Grateful children must love their mothers; Beethoven loved his greatly.

Outside the physical body, during the hours of sleep, the soul can talk to her Divine Mother. We must, however, begin with dream yoga discipline.

We need to take care of the bedroom where we sleep; it must be pleasantly decorated. The colors best suited for the goal we seek, in spite of what other authors recommend, are precisely the three primary hues: blue, yellow and red. The three basic colors constantly correspond to the three primary forces of Nature, the Holy Triamatzicamno: Holy Affirmation, Holy Negation, and Holy Conciliation.[23] It is worth remembering that the three original forces of this great creation always crystallize in the positive, negative, and neutral forms. The causa causarum of the Holy Triamatzicamno is found hidden in the active element Okidanokh.[24] The latter, in and of itself, is only the emanation of the sacred solar Absolute.[25] Obviously, the rejection of the three fundamental colors, having given the above explanations, is equivalent, by simple logical deduction, to become a nonsensical foolishness.

Dream yoga is extraordinary, marvelous, and formidable. It is, however, very demanding.

The bedroom has to be always very well perfumed and ventilated, but not pervaded with the cold dew of the night.

After undergoing detailed and careful preparation of himself for bed and of the room where he will sleep, a

23 The law of nature through which action is accomplished, by means of three forces.
24 The Ray of Creation.
25 See glossary.

Gnostic must take care of his bed. If we observe any compass, we can see that the needle always points to the north. Unquestionably, it is then possible to consciously take advantage of the planet's magnetic current, which always flows from south to north. A bed should be placed in such a way that the head is facing north. In this way, we can intelligently use the magnetic current indicated by the needle. The mattress should be neither too hard nor too soft. This means that its texture must in no way affect the psychic processes of the sleeping person. Squeaking bedsprings or a base that cracks with every small movement of the body are serious obstacles for these practices.

A pad or notebook and a pencil should be placed under the pillow so that they can easily be found, even in the dark.

Bedclothes must be fresh and clean; the pillowcase must be scented with our favorite perfume.

After having met these requirements, the ascetic Gnostic will be ready for the second stage of this esoteric discipline.

He will get into bed, and having turned off all the lights, will lay on his back with his eyes closed and place both hands on his solar plexus.

He will be totally quiet for some time, and once he is completely relaxed physically as well as mentally, he will concentrate on Morpheus, the god of sleep.

Unquestionably, each part of our real Being has specific tasks. It is precisely Morpheus (do not confuse with Orpheus) who is in charge of training us in the mysteries of sleep.

It is impossible to trace a layout of our Being. Nevertheless, all the spiritual, isolated parts of the Being want to achieve absolute perfection in their tasks.

Morpheus enjoys this unique opportunity we provide when we concentrate on him.

We must know how to supplicate and have faith. We have to ask Morpheus to teach us and to awaken us in the suprasensible worlds.

By this time, the esotericist Gnostic feels a very special somnolence, and then adopts the "lion posture." Lie on your right side with your head pointing north, and move your legs slowly so that your knees are bent. In this posture, the left leg rests on top of the right one. Then place

your right cheek on your right palm and
let your left arm rest on your left leg.

When one wakes up, one should not
move, because any movement shakes up
our "values" and then the memory of our
dreams is lost.

Undoubtedly, in those moments
when we want to remember our dream or
dreams with complete precision, a retrospective exercise becomes indispensable.

The Gnostics have to take notes,
carefully, of the details of their dream or
dreams in the notebook or pad which
they placed under their pillow. In this
way, they will be able to have a detailed
record of their inner progress in dream
yoga.

Even if there are only vague fragments
of the dream or dreams in our memory,
these must be thoroughly recorded.

When nothing is left in the memory, the retrospective exercise must be
based on the first thought we had at the
moment we awakened. That thought,
obviously, relates to the last dream.

We must point out that the retrospective exercise should start before completely coming back to the vigil state, when we

are still drowsy, to try to follow the dream sequence.

The practice of that exercise always starts with the last image that we had moments before coming back to the vigil state.

We will conclude this chapter with the serious statement that it is not possible to go beyond this stage of the dream yoga discipline unless we have obtained the perfect memory of our dream experiences.

Special Nourishment to Develop the Power of the Memory

Prepare your breakfast with acid fruits and ground almonds along with honey (bee honey). In this way you will provide the brain with the necessary atoms for the memory.

Chapter 7
Tantric Dream

Undoubtedly, to review our pad or notebook every month in order to verify the gradual progression of our dream memory is appropriate.

Any possibility of forgetting a dream must be eliminated. We cannot continue further with practices unless we have achieved perfect memory.

Of particular interest are those dreams which seem to come from past centuries, or that unfold in environments totally unrelated to the vigil existence of the dreamer.

One must be in a "watchful, perceptive" or "alert, anew" state and pay attention to the study of details which includes specific matters, conversations, meetings, temples, or unusual activities which relate to other people.

Once the total development of the dream memory is achieved, and any possibility of lack of memory is eliminated, the symbolism process will open the way to revelation.

We must seek the basic science of interpretation of dreams in the law of philosophical analogies, the law of the opposite analogies, and the law of correspondences and numerology.

The astral images reflected in the magical mirror of imagination can never be translated literally, for these are only the symbolic representation of archetypal ideas. They must be utilized in the same way as a mathematician uses algebraic symbols.

It is not irrelevant to affirm that such ideas come down from the pure world of the Spirit.

The archetypal ideas descending from the Being are marvelous, for they inform us about the psychological status of any center of the human machine, about esoteric or intimate matters, or about possible successes or dangers, etc. These are always wrapped in the marvelous cover of symbolism.

It is possible to unveil any of the astral symbols, scenes, or figures, with the goal of taking out their essential ideas, only by means of the comparative and logical meditation of the Being.

On reaching this stage of dream yoga discipline, it is indispensable to approach the tantric[26] aspect of the matter.

Ancient wisdom teaches that Tonantzin (Devi Kundalini), our divine, cosmic, individual Mother (each of us has our own), can take any form, for she is the origin of all forms. Therefore, it is convenient for the Gnostic to meditate upon her before falling asleep.

The candidate will start the dreaming process by repeating daily with great faith the following prayer:

"Tonantzin, Teteoinan! My Mother, come to me, come to me!"

According to tantric science, if the Gnostic persists with this practice, sooner or later an initiator element will come forth amongst the changing and formless expressions of one's dreams.

As long as this initiator has not been totally identified, it is indispensable to continue recording dreams on the pad or notebook.

---

26 In Asian mysticism, tantra is the class of teachings that was traditionally reserved for the most qualified and serious students. See glossary.

The study and profound analysis of every recorded dream becomes indispensable in tantric dream esoteric discipline.

This didactic progression will lead us to the discovery of the initiator or unifier element of dreams.

Undoubtedly, the sincere Gnostic who reaches this stage of tantric discipline is, for this reason, ready for the next step, which will be the topic of our next chapter.

Chapter 8
The Return Practice

When the aspirant has successfully performed all of the Gnostic exercises related with the esotericism of dreams, then it is evident one is intimately prepared for the "return practice."

In the previous chapter, we mentioned the initiator element that comes forth as if by enchantment from amongst the changing and formless expressions of dreams.

Certain people, who are highly psychic, refined or susceptible to impressions, have always possessed in themselves the initiator element. These people are characterized by the continuous repetition of the same dream. These psychics periodically re-live various scenes, or constantly see in their dream experience a creature or a symbol...

Every time the aspirant wakes up from ordinary sleep and remembers the initiator element (be it a symbol, a sound, a color, a person, etc.), he keeps his eyes closed and goes on with the visualization of that familiar image. He will then try to go back to sleep to continue the same dream. In other words, the aspirant tries to be conscious of his own dream; that is why he intentionally goes on with it, but carries it to the vigil state in full lucidity and self-control. Hence, he becomes a spectator and actor of a dream with the advantage, certainly not insignificant, of being able to abandon the scene at will in order to move freely in the astral world. Then the aspirant, free of the limitations of the flesh, outside the physical body, will have discarded his old familiar environment and penetrated a universe ruled by different laws.

The discipline of the dream state of Tantric Buddhists methodically leads us to the awakening of our consciousness.

Gnostics can awaken to the real state of illumination only through the comprehension and elimination of dreams.

Sacred scriptures from Hindustan solemnly assert that the whole world is Brahma's dream. Having this Hindu postulate as a base, let us emphasize that, "when Brahma awakens, his dream ends."

As long as the aspirant does not achieve the radical dissolution, not only of dreams, but also of the psychological roots that originate them, absolute awakening is impossible.

The definite awakening of the consciousness is possible only by means of a radical transformation.

The four Christic gospels insist on the necessity of awakening. Unfortunately, people are still sleeping.

Quetzalcoatl, the Mexican Christ, was certainly a human being who was one hundred percent awakened. The multiplicity of his attributes points to us precisely the antiquity of his cult and the profound veneration he received in Mesoamerica.

The holy gods of Anahuac[27] are perfect humans in the strictest sense of the word. They are absolutely awakened. Those beings eradicated even the possibility of dreams from their psyche.

Tlaloc, "he who makes sprouting," the god of the rain and lightning, being a god, is also an awakened human who had to eliminate from his psyche not only his dreams, but also all possibilities of dreaming. He is the principal sacred individual of the ancient Olmec culture. He is always

---

27   The ancient name of the Valley of Mexico.

depicted with the tiger-serpent's mask in colossal axes and various jade figures.

Tezcatlipoca and Huitzilopochtli, creatures of the fire, living representations of night and day, are also awakened humans, beings who went beyond their dreams.

Out of the physical body, an awakened individual can invoke the holy gods of the Aztecs, Mayans, Zapotecs, Toltecs, and others.

The gods of the Borgia, Borbon, and other codices come to help those who awaken.

By means of the help of the holy gods, the awakened person can study the secret doctrine of Anahuac in the Astral Light.

Chapter 9

The Four Blessings

In the last chapter, we referred extensively to the initiator element of dreams. Obviously, we only lack the ability to use it.

When the Gnostic has kept a record of his dreams, he unquestionably discovers a dream that recurs. This, among other reasons, certainly justifies writing all dreams in his notebook or pad.

Undoubtedly, that recurring dream experience is the initiator element which, wisely used, leads us to the awakening of the consciousness.

Every time the mystic lies on the bed, goes to sleep and meditates at will on the initiator element, the result is immediate.

Usually, the anchorite re-lives such dreams consciously, and is able to leave the scene at will, to travel in the suprasensible worlds.

Any dream can be used for such purposes when we actually know the technique.

Whoever awakens from a dream can continue with it intentionally if desiring

to do so. In this case, one must go back
to sleep and re-live that dream experience
with imagination.

We must not imagine that we are
imagining.

Fundamentally, we should re-live the
dream in its full and crude reality.

Repeating the dream intentionally is
the first step towards the awakening of
the consciousness. The voluntary separation from the dream, in plain action, is
the second step.

Some aspirants take the first step, but
they lack the strength to take the second
one. Such people can and should help
themselves by means of the technique of
meditation.

By making serious decisions, those
devotees will practice meditation before
going to sleep.

The motive of concentration and
reflection in their inner and deep meditation will be, in this case, their inner situation...

In this practice, the mystic, in sor-
row, feeling sincere emotion, will invoke
their Divine Mother Tonantzin (Devi
Kundalini).

Shedding tears of pain, the ascetic Gnostic will lament their state of unconsciousness, and will implore for help, beseeching their Divine Mother for strength to detach at will from any dream.

The goal this tantric dream discipline seeks is to prepare the disciple to clearly recognize the four blessings that manifest in the dream experience.

This esoteric discipline is certainly only for very serious people, for it demands infinite patience and enormous inner super-efforts.

A lot has been said in Asia about the four lights[28] of the dream state; let us study this matter.

The first one is called the "Revealing Light." It is written in gold letters in the book of life that this is perceived just before, or during the first hours of sleep.

Speaking frankly and to the point, let us point out that, as sleep becomes deeper, the undesirable melding of residual impressions and the usual train of dis-

---

28 In Tibetan tantra, the first three lights or luminosity are described as modes of self-awareness (light, increase of light, and culmination of light), and are also called three consciousnesses. The fourth is the state of the primordial unconditioned consciousness.

criminatory thoughts fortunately dissolve slowly.

In this stage of sleep, the second illumination progressively shows. This is known in Asia by the marvelous name of "Increasing Light."

Unquestionably, by means of the extraordinary tantric dream discipline, the Gnostic ascetic gets beyond this stage and apprehends the two remaining lights.

To vividly experience the crude reality of practical life in the superior worlds of cosmic consciousness signifies the acquisition of the third light, "the Immediate Realization."

The fourth light is that of the "Inner Profound Illumination," and it comes to us as if by enchantment in plain mystical experience.

"Here, in the fourth degree of the void, dwells the child of the Mother Clear Light," states a Tibetan treatise.

Frankly speaking and without ambiguities, I declare the following: the tantric dream discipline is in fact an esoteric preparation for that final dream that we call death.

Having "died" many times at night, the Gnostic anchorite who has consciously apprehended the four blessings that present themselves in the dreaming experience, passes to the postmortem state when he dies with the same ease manner that he willingly gets into the world of dreams.

Outside his physical body, the Gnostic can consciously verify for himself the fate reserved to the souls beyond death.

If, every night, by means of the tantric dream discipline, the esotericist can consciously "die" and enter into the world of the dead, it is evident that he will then be able as well to, "study the ritual of life and death while the officiant arrives...."

After he visited the infernos, where he saw in horror the fate of the lost souls, Hermes became acquainted with unknown facts...

> "Look to that side (Osiris tells Hermes). Do you see that hive of souls who try to climb up to the lunar region? Some are rushed down to the ground, just like flocks of birds under the blows of a storm. The other ones, with the strokes of their wings, reach the superior sphere,

which pulls them on its rotation. Once they reach there, they recover the sight of divine things."

When burying those chosen by Tlaloc, the rain god, the Aztecs placed a dried branch nearby. It was said that, when the blessed one reached the Field of Delights, or Tlalocan, the dried branch turned green again indicating in this way the return to a new life...

Those who have not been chosen by the Sun or Tlaloc fatally go to Mictlan, which is in the north, a region where the souls undergo a series of magical trials on passing through the infernal worlds.

There are nine places where the souls suffer unbearably before reaching the final rest. This reminds us, in an emphatic way, of the nine infernal circles of Dante Alighieri's *Divine Comedy*.

Many are the gods and goddesses who populate the nine Dantean circles of the Aztec inferno.

It is worthwhile to remember in this 1974-1975 Christmas Message the frightful Mictlantecuhtli and the tenebrous Mictecacihuatl, the lord and lady of the infernos [respectively], inhabitants of the ninth and deepest underground of those places.

The souls who undergo the trials of the Aztec inferno later, after the "second death,"[29] enter joyfully the paradises of the elementals of Nature.

Unquestionably, those souls who neither descend to the infernal worlds after death, nor ascend to the Kingdom of the Golden Light, or to Tlaloc's paradise, or the Kingdom of Eternal Concentration, etc., will come back or return sooner or later to a new physical body.

The souls chosen by the Sun or Tlaloc rejoice much in the superior worlds before returning to this vale of samsara.

The Gnostic anchorites, after having grasped the four lights of dreams, can consciously visit the Tlalocan every night, or go down to the Mictlan, or contact those souls who, before returning, still live in the lunar region.

---

29 See glossary.

Our guardian angel

Chapter 10

The Guardian Angel

The first educator of any great initiate is in fact and by its own right the fundamental cause of all his spiritualized parts of his genuine common presence.

Any grateful guru humbly prostrates before the first creator of his genuine Being.

After many conscious works and voluntary sufferings, the absolute perfection achieved in the functioning of all the spiritualized, isolated parts of our common presence is revealed before our tearful eyes. Then, the Being's impulse of gratitude towards the first educator emerges from within us.

Unquestionably, the absolute perfection of each and every isolated part of the Being can be achieved only by radically dying in ourselves here and now.

There are various stages of inner Self-realization.

Some initiates have achieved perfection in some isolated parts of their Being, nonetheless they still have much work to do before reaching absolute perfection of all parts.

It would be in no way possible to portray the Being. It resembles an army of innocent children; each of them performs specific tasks. The greatest longing of all initiates is to achieve the total integration of all parts of the Being.

When one achieves the inner Self-realization of the highest part of one's Being, one receives the grade "Ishmesch."

Our Lord Quetzalcoatl, the Mexican Christ, undoubtedly developed the highest part of his Being. It should be noted that Xolotl, the Nahua Lucifer, is also one of our Being's isolated parts.

The elemental gods of Nature — such as Huehueteotl, Tlaloc, Ehecatl, Chalciutlicue (Tlaloc's Genevieve), Xochiquetzal, the goddess of flowers, etc. — assist the initiate in his elemental magic operations, provided that there is upright behavior.

Nevertheless, we should not forget our elemental intercessor, the elemental magician in each of us who can invoke the elemental gods of Nature and perform prodigies. This is unquestionably another one of the Being's isolated parts.

The three goddesses Tonantzin, Coatlicue, and Tlazolteotl are only three aspects of the same divinity, variations or derivations of our own Being, representing our Divine Mother.

Our Being has many isolated parts.

One becomes astounded when remembering the lion of the law, the two genii who take note of our good and bad deeds, the karmic police, a part of our Being as well, the All-Merciful, the Compassionate One, our united Father-Mother, and the guardian angel, etc.

The flaming powers of the guardian angel are truly extraordinary, marvelous, and extremely divine. I know what the guardian angel is from purely Gnostic sources, secretly kept in monasteries of initiation. These bear no resemblance to common pseudo-Christianity and pseudo-occultism that are accessible to the general public.

On reaching the very mysterious field of the history and the life of the jinns, we have discovered not only the Chapultepec Temple in Mexico and the people from the fourth vertical, but also, to our amazement, the power of the guardian angel and its relationship with all this.

Let us never forget Padre Prado and Bernal Diaz del Castillo who, together, observed with delight the Anahuac priests in jinn states.

The anchorites floated delightfully through the air and went from Cholula to the Templo Mayor. This happened every day at sunset. Never in their nocturnal walks did the Sais' disciples in the delta of the Nile, or Zaratustra's followers in the Persian plateaux, or those who meditated in Belo's Tower in Babylonia, have more majestic horizons than the ones that are observed by those who seriously persevere in tantric dream discipline.

Outside the physical body, the Gnostic anchorite can consciously, if one wills it, invoke an isolated part of one's Being, which is defined in practical esotericism with the name of guardian angel. Unquestionably, the Ineffable will heed his call.

In such delightful moments we feel transparent serenity, limitless calm, or ecstatic happiness, like that which is experienced by the soul when breaking the bonds of matter and the world.

You can then, dear reader, deduce the outcome: magical services a la *Lohengrin*[30] can always be received.

If, in such rapturous moments, we ask of the guardian angel the favor of removing our body, which is sleeping in bed where we left it, and bringing it to us, the magical phenomenon will take place successfully.

We can sense that the physical body is on its way, brought by the guardian angel, when we feel a strange pressure on our psychic or astral shoulders.

If we assume a receptive, open and quiet attitude, the physical body will penetrate our interior.

The tantric gnostic, instead of returning to his physical body, consciously waits for it to come to him in order to travel to the Promised Land in the fourth coordinate.

Later, with the help of the guardian angel, the gnostic can safely go back home to bed.

The venerable masters of the esoteric fraternity travel with their physical bodies in the fourth vertical, and can leave the fourth vertical at any point they wish.

---

30 Richard Wagner's opera.

This means that the resurrected masters of the superior order have the luxury of transporting themselves without modern transportation systems, boats, airplanes or cars; not a trivial matter.

In ancient times, the use of criticism, analogy, and symbology were the living core of the Alexandrian school of the Philaleteans or "truth lovers," a sixth century academy of synthesis founded by Ammonio Saccas, the great autodidact and eclectic, and Plotinus, Plato's follower.

Throughout the centuries, the great initiatic value of these procedures and the doctrinal principles of Egypt, Mexico, Peru, China, Tibet, Persia, and India helped many initiates orient themselves in the path of the razor's edge. Ammonio Sacas' *Androgilia* is remarkable; it is an excellent, golden book.

Self-aggrandizement is the biggest error that many modern pseudo-esotericists and pseudo-occultists have. They love themselves so much, and they yearn for the evolution of the misery they carry within. They want to move on and long for the extension of that which in no way deserves either perfection or perpetuation.

Those people with subjective psyches believe themselves to be rich, powerful, and illuminated. They covet a splendid position in the beyond. In reality, they know nothing about themselves.

Lamentably, they are ignorant of their own impotence, nothingness, shamelessness, misadventures, and psychological misery and nakedness.

We Gnostics do not yearn to be better or worse; we only want to die in ourselves here and now.

When we have the dogma of "evolution" as the foundation of our most cherished yearnings, our point of departure is false.

We, the penitents of the rocky path that leads to final liberation, are not interested in evolution. We know we are miserable and crippled, and our own evolution would be useless. We prefer supreme death; only death brings forth what is new...

Why should we struggle for the evolution and progression of our own misfortune? It is better to die.

If the seed does not die, the plant cannot sprout. When death is absolute, that which will be born will also be absolute.

Total annihilation of the self, the radical dissolution of the most loved which we carry within, the final disintegration of our best desires, thoughts, feelings, passions, resentments, sorrows, emotions, yearnings, hatred, likings, jealousy, revenge, anger, affections, attachments, passion, lust, is urgent and undelayable, it cannot be postponed. In this way, the Being's flame, which is always new and does not belong to time, can come forth...

The conception we have of the Being is not the Being. Any intellectual concept we have created about the Being is not the Being. Our opinion of the Being is not the Being. The Being is the Being, and the reason for the Being to be is to be itself.

Fear of absolute death is an obstacle to the realization of radical change.

Each of us has a mistaken creation in our interior. It is essential to destroy what is false so that a new creation can come forth. We would never try to promote the evolution of falseness; we prefer an absolute annihilation.

From the black and horrifying sepulchral grave of the abyss, arise the diverse flaming parts of the Being. The guardian angel is one of those many isolated parts.

Those who really know the mysteries of the Templars, which are a marvelous reflection of Bacchian, Eleusian, and Pythagorean mysteries, by no means wish to carry on their inner misery.

We ought to return to the original point of departure. We must go back to the primeval darkness of the Not-Being and Chaos, so that light can be born and a new creation can come forth in our interior.

Instead of fearing total annihilation, it is better to learn how to love and fall into the arms of our Blessed Goddess Mother Death.

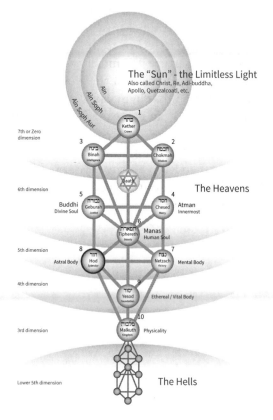

The "Sun" - the Limitless Light
Also called Christ, Re, Adi-buddha, Apollo, Quetzalcoatl, etc.

7th or Zero dimension

6th dimension   The Heavens

5th dimension

4th dimension

3rd dimension

Lower 5th dimension   The Hells

Ain
Ain Soph
Ain Soph Aur

1 כתר Kether Crown
3 בינה Binah Intelligence
2 חכמה Chokmah Wisdom
Daath
5 גבורה Geburah Justice — Buddhi Divine Soul
4 חסד Chesed Mercy — Atman Innermost
6 תפארת Tiphereth Beauty — Manas Human Soul
8 הוד Hod Splendor — Astral Body
7 נצח Netzach Victory — Mental Body
9 יסוד Yesod Foundation — Ethereal / Vital Body
10 מלכות Malkuth Kingdom — Physicality

KABBALAH, THE TREE OF LIFE

Chapter 11
Hod

Hod[31] is the astral world, the astral body. The astral world is governed by the Moon. This is why astral projections become easier during the waxing moon and a little bit more arduous during the waning moon.

The astral plane is really the plane of practical magic. For example, in some of the tribes of the most profound jungles of the amazons, the piaches or sorcerer-priests give unto their people a special beverage in order to enter into the astral plane at will. They mix the ashes of a tree called guarumo with very well-ground leaves of coca. This is administered when the Moon is crescent; thus this is how the astral projection is performed. The Piaches know very well that Hod, the astral world, is governed by the Moon, but many Kabbalists suppose that it is governed by Mercury and they are mistaken.[32]

---

31 Hebrew הוד means "glory, majesty, splendor," and in Kabbalah is the eighth sephirah of the Tree of Life.

32 This is explained in *Tarot and Kabbalah* by Samael Aun Weor.

The messages that descend from the world of the pure Spirit become symbolic in the astral plane. Those symbols are interpreted based on the law of philosophical analogies, on the law of analogous contraries, on the law of correspondences, and on the law of numerology. In order to learn how to interpret your astral experiences, the book of Daniel and the biblical passages of the Patriarch Joseph, son of Jacob, must be studied.

The legitimate and authentic astral body is the solar astral body. The body of desires,[33] which is of a lunar nature,[34] has been mistakenly called the astral body.

All of the creatures of nature are lunar. They possess a lunar astral body, which is a cold protoplasmatic body, a bestial remnant of the past.

What we need is to build the authentic body of Hod, the legitimate astral body, which is a vehicle of a solar nature. This must be built in the Ninth Sphere[35]

---

33 Sanskrit, kama rupa.
34 See glossary.
35 In Kabbalah, a reference to the sephirah Yesod of the Tree of Life (Kabbalah). When you place the Tree of Life over your body, you see that Yesod is related to your sexual organs. "The Ninth Sphere of the Kabbalah is sex." —Samael Aun Weor, The Perfect Matrimony

by working in the flaming forge of Vulcan.[36]

The solar astral body is a body of flesh and bone that does not come from Adam. It is a body that eats, digests, and assimilates.

There are diverse authors of a pseudo-esoteric and pseudo-occult type that fall into the error of mistaking the ego with the astral body.

Modern metaphysical literature speaks a lot about projections of the astral body, although we must have the courage to recognize that fans of esotericism are accustomed to projecting themselves with their ego in order to travel in the sublunar regions of nature through time and space.

With the solar astral body we can travel through the Milky Way towards the central sun Sirius. To go beyond the Milky Way is forbidden unto us, because in the other galaxies there are other types of cosmic laws that are unknown to the inhabitants of this galaxy.

There is a great temple in Sirius where the great masters of this galaxy receive ini-

36 Latin name of the god of fire who makes the armor and weapons of the heroes. See glossary.

tiation. The disciples of the God Sirius are Rosicrucian Gnostics; the true Rosi-Cross is in the superior worlds. The disciples of the Rosi-Cross have the Holy Grail emblazoned on their hoods. They also celebrate the drama of the Christ, because it is a cosmic drama.

Our disciples must acquire the power of travelling with the astral body. This power is acquired by daily vocalizing for an hour the sacred mantra **Egipto**.[37] The vowel "E" makes the thyroid gland vibrate and grants unto the person the power of the occult ear. The "G" awakes the chakra of the liver, and when this chakra has reached its complete development the person can enter and depart from the physical body whenever it is wished. The "I", when combined with the letter "P" develops clairvoyance and the power to leave in the astral body through the window of Brahma, which is the pineal gland. The letter "T" beats upon the vowel "O," which is intimately related with the chakra of the heart. Thus, the human being can acquire the power in order to

---

37   Pronounced with E as the eh in "they," G as in "good," I as the ee in "tree," O as the oh in "holy."

detach from this plexus and depart in the astral body.

The correct pronunciation of the mantra **Egipto** is as follows:

Eeeeeeggggggiiiiiiiiiiptoooooo

Some still do not attain the capacity of departing in the astral body with other clues because they do not have that power. Then they must acquire this power, firstly, by vocalizing for one hour daily the mantra Egipto. This mantra completely develops the chakras related with the projection of the astral body. This is how the disciple acquires the power of astral projection. The disciple could then enter and leave the body at will.

The Egyptian mantra that is utilized in order to depart in the astral body is the following: **FARAON**.[38] This mantra is vocalized in those instances of transition between vigil and dream, having the mind concentrated on the pyramids of Egypt.

The correct pronunciation of the mantra **FARAON** is as follows:

---

38 Pronounced with A as the ah in "father." O as the oh in "holy"

Faaaaarrrrraaaaooooonnnn

This mantra is used in order to depart in the astral body and, as we have already stated, it is pronounced during the state of transition between vigil and dream with the mind concentrated on the pyramids of Egypt. Nonetheless, the disciples that do not have the power of departing with the astral body must first acquire it by vocalizing daily for one hour the mantra **Egipto**.

Chapter 12

The Science of Meditation

We are going to talk about the science of meditation. But first we should prepare ourselves in a positive manner in order to receive this type of superior teaching to take advantage of time. This is the moment for us to understand the need of giving more opportunity to our consciousness.

Normally we live on different levels of our interior temple. There are people who always live in the lower levels; those are the ones that are concentrated exclusively in instinct and fornication, the fourth and fifth levels (instinctive and sexual centers, respectively), levels that have been used in a negative way.

Others live on the third level (motor center) and never leave it; they always

Intellectual

Motor

Emotional

Instinctual

Sexual

move following the patterns of predeter-
mined customs, along the line of certain
habits. They never change; they are like
a train that always runs over the same
tracks. These third-level types of people
are so accustomed to their train of habits
that they are not ready to surrender them.

Others live on the first level (the intellectual center); others, on the second level
(negative emotions). Those who live in
the intellectual center want to turn everything into rationalism, analysis, concepts,
or arguments, and they never leave that
place.

Others live in the emotional center
dedicated to the vices of movies, race-
tracks, bullfights, etc.; in reality, a very
limited and narrow world. They live
enclosed and enslaved by negative emotions, never thinking of escaping from
such places.

It is necessary to insist upon giving
opportunity to our consciousness.

There are different types of dreams:
intellectual and emotional dreams, others
that belong to the motor center or sexual center, or others that are exclusively
related to sexual activities. These types of
dreams always reflect situations lived dur-

ing the day; they are repetitions of daily activities.

If people live on the emotional levels, their dreams will reflect situations of terror or craziness; if they live on the sexual level, their dreams will be of lust, adultery, fornication, masturbation, etc. If the dreams belong to the instinctive center, they become incoherent, so submerged that it is impossible to understand them.

Each of the five centers of the human machine produces certain types of dreams. Truly we have to say that only the dreams that belong to the superior emotional center (seventh level) are the ones to which we must give attention. The same can be applied to the positive aspect of the sixth center (superior mental center). Dreams from any of the inferior centers (the instinctive, motor, sexual, emotional, or intellectual) do not have any importance.

We need to be able to distinguish from which center the dream is coming. This is only possible by knowing the activities of each of the five centers of the human machine. Dreams from the superior emotional center are the most important because in them we find perfect, organized dramas, in accordance with the daily activities of our consciousness if we give it the opportunity to work.

What happens is that the Ray of Creation from which we emanated constructs everything from the superior emotional center. It is from there that diverse superior parts of our Being, related with the Ray of Creation, are manifested through this center in order to instruct us during our hours of sleep; then well organized, clear, and precise scenes are presented to us so we will be able to understand our situation, our errors and defects, etc.

Of course, the language of the superior emotional center is symbolic, allegoric, and corresponds to the Hermetic Kabbalah, to Hermenetics, etc. Unquestionably, it is through this center that any person dedicated to esoteric studies can receive correct and precise information.

We have taught you to sleep on your back with your head toward the north, relaxing the body and praying (supplicating) to Divine Mother Kundalini to give you esoteric instructions. We have also taught you the need to lie down on your right side in the lion posture.

When you tire of the right side, you can switch to the left side, keeping the lion posture. Once the disciple wakes up, he should not move but should try to do the retrospective exercise in order to remember all the dream experiences until they are imprinted and registered clearly in his brain and memory. But I want to clarify that not all dreams are important.

For example, pornographic sexual dreams, erotic dreams with nocturnal emissions, are dreams of an inferior nature.

Also, instinctive, motor dreams do not have importance because they are only reflections of one's daily activities.

Dreams related to the lower emotional center do not have importance because they are of a passionate, brutal type.

Intellectual dreams are only projections and are also of no value at all.

I repeat, only those related to the higher emotional center should be considered; but in addition, we need to understand the meaning of our dreams in order to avoid mistakes.

It is necessary to interpret the allegoric messages received through the superior emotional center, because those are the teachings coming from the White Brotherhood or from the superior part of our Being. This makes us see the urgent necessity of understanding the profound meaning of all symbolism that should be deciphered in a very precise way in accordance to our development.

After all clarification in relation to dreams, I should tell you we urgently need to pass through the dream or astral world to become awake in the inner superior worlds. This is possible only when we give greater opportunities to our consciousness.

Normally people act and react in response to the impacts coming from the outer world. Compare this to the example of a lake in which we throw a stone; we see how the stone produces rings that spread from the center to the edge of the lake. This is the reaction of the water to the impact coming from the stone (external world). Something similar happens to the mind and feelings. If someone hurts us with words, the impact of the word reaches the intellectual center or the

thought center and then the person reacts
in a violent way; if someone offends our
senses, we feel annoyed and possibly react
in a brutish way.

In every circumstance of life the mind
and feelings take an active part reacting
consecutively (in response to the external
stimulus). A better response would be not
to give any opportunity to the mind or
feelings; it is urgent to develop a tranquil,
quiet mind. This of course bothers the
"mentalists" everywhere.

The idea of a quiet mind is opposed
to all those who say that "in the mind is
the power" and that "man must be a king
who commands and dominates with his
powerful mind." These are sophisms of
the mentalists, like those who say, "He
who learns to manage his mind is sure to
triumph like the arrow of the old archer."
Finally, at the very end, they are nothing
more than sophisms extracted from those
intellectual fantasies which have no esoteric form.

To negate thinking—this horrifies
the mind positivists, but nevertheless
the negated form of the mind is the
most eloquent. Not thinking is the most
elevated way of thinking. When the think-

ing process of the mind is concluded, the new way arrives; this is what you need to understand.

A calm mind that is at the service of one's real Being results in an efficient instrument, because the mind is made to be receptive, to serve as a receptive instrument, not as an active instrument. The mind itself is feminine, and all the centers should work harmoniously in accordance with the universal symphony of passive serenity. In these conditions we should not permit the mind to project; we need a tranquil mind to put to the service of the different circumstances of our existence.

Until a short time ago, I myself thought that emotions or sentiments came from the real Being, but with investigation and experience I have come to verify that they pertain to the ego and that they are intimately related to the inferior emotional center.

The therapy we need to know profoundly in order to avoid any interior unbalance that can cause outer repercussions is that which will not permit the mind any kind of reaction. If someone hurts us, we must not permit the mind to react. Wish that there will always be someone who can hurt us in our feelings daily, so that we can in that way train our mind better to be passive. The more insults we receive, the better for our training, because we will have more opportunities to stop the reaction of the mind and feelings so that they do not intervene in any circumstance of our lives.

Of course, the passive state of mind, emotions, and personality demands a tremendous activity in the consciousness; this shows us that the more active the consciousness, the better for reaching its awakening, because that way the consciousness has to inevitably awaken, being in perpetual activity.

Just now, Buddha Gautama Shakyamuni came to my mind. On a certain occasion, the great Buddha was sitting under a tree in profound meditation when a man arrived and began to insult the Buddha, trying to hurt him with his words.

After a while, the Buddha opened his eyes and asked the man, "If someone brings you a gift and you do not accept the gift, to whom does this gift belong?"

The man answered, "To the one who brought it, of course."

Buddha Gautama Shakyamuni

Then the Buddha said, "My brother, take your gift; I cannot accept it," and continued to meditate.

This is a beautiful, sublime lesson. Buddha did not permit his mind or sentiments to react under any circumstances because he was living fully awakened in his consciousness; there was no outer reaction. That is the way we should behave, dear disciples.

The school is everywhere; we have to take advantage of it and learn wisely. We have it in our houses, our offices, the shops, or factories, in the street... everywhere, even in the temple, with our fellow students, our children, father, wife, nephews, grandsons, cousins, friends, etc. All are psychological gymnasiums. As hard as it will be, as difficult as it looks to us, it is indispensable for all of us. The secret is not to allow our mind and feelings to intervene in the practical daily activities of our lives.

We should allow the consciousness to be the one who commands, directs, and works, the one who talks and executes all one's daily activities. That way we prepare harmoniously for meditation.

From the practical point of meditation, we must say that what we are looking for goes beyond mind and feelings. This is only possible if in our practical daily life we have trained ourselves intensively and prepared ourselves in our daily lives for this wonderful goal.

Meditation becomes difficult when in our daily life we have not passed through a rigorous training, when we have not trained properly in the psychological gymnasium using social and family life as a training field.

During meditation, we should release the Essence, the Buddhata,[39] the best inside of us, the most dignified and decent. Precisely the Essence or Buddhata is enclosed within the inhuman elements or psychological aggregates that constitute the "I" or ego.

It is not possible to experience reality or truth, that which interests all of us, unless we free the Essence, which is trapped in the ego; if we do not, we will have to continue to live on in a world of dreams, in the intellectual center, emotional center, motor center, instinctive,

---

39 That element in us that has the potential to become a Buddha, an "awakened one."

or the sexual centers. We want to be able to escape, to experience truth. The great Kabir Jesus said:

> *"And ye shall know the truth, and the truth shall make you free."* –John 8:32

Truth is not a question of theories; it is not a question of believing or not believing. It is not a matter of concepts or opinions.

Can you form opinions in relation to truth?

What is an opinion? It is the projection of a concept, hiding the doubt and fear that truth is something else.

What is a concept? Simply an elaborated reasoning projected by the mind; it may or may not coincide with something.

Can we assume that a concept or an opinion given out by the intellect would be precisely the truth? No.

What is an idea? An idea can be magnificent; for example we can form an idea in relation to the Sun; such an idea could be more or less exact, or more or less mistaken, but they are not the Sun. That way also we could form multiple ideas in relation to truth but they are not the truth.

When Jesus Christ was asked what is truth he kept silence; when Gautama Shakyamuni the Buddha received the same question, he turned and walked away. Truth cannot be defined by words; the same with a sunset. Anyone can go into ecstasy while watching the Sun beginning to hide behind the golden splendor of the mountains, but trying to communicate to others this mystical experience is very difficult because others will not feel the same.

So, truth cannot be communicated. Truth is real for the one who has the experience. When freed of the ego we can experience truth, we can perceive a radical transforming element within us as a high voltage element. This is possible but we have to know how to get it: by putting to work our consciousness to replace mind and feeling so that the integrated consciousness in us will be the one to function.

We must have a passive intellect, a passive emotional center, and a passive personality, but have a totally active consciousness. To understand this is indispensable; it is urgent if we are to become practical meditators.

Meditation

With the technique of meditation what we are looking for is information. With a microscope we can see the life of microbes, bacteria, cells, microorganisms, etc. Any telescope can give us information about the celestial bodies, planets, meteorites, stars, etc. But meditation goes beyond and can allow us to know the truth from something so small to something as grand as the Sun, the truth of an atom or a constellation.

The most important thing is to learn to know how we can disentangle, take out our consciousness from our mind and ego, to know how to extract the consciousness from within the emotions. When we dominate the mind and emotions, obviously, we are breaking chains; we are coming out of that deadly dungeon, of that jail. In this way, we are preparing ourselves for meditation.

Before anything we have to know how to meditate, we have to learn the correct technique. In the Asian world they put a lot of emphasis on the padmasana position with the legs crossed, but we are not Asian and should meditate in accordance with our own customs and style. As a matter of fact, not all the Asians meditate with their legs crossed. What is important is that each person should adopt the position best for him. If you want to meditate with your legs crossed, do it; we are not going to prohibit this, but this is not the only practical position for meditation.

For a correct meditation we can take a seat in a comfortable chair, with arms and legs relaxed, without tension in our muscles; or if you wish, you can lie down and take the position of the five pointed star (hands and legs open to each side) with one's head toward the north. Remember, you can take any form or position you like or the most comfortable for you.

If in reality we want to separate our consciousness from our mind, emotions, and the psychological "I," it does not matter which position we take. The important thing is to know how to meditate; do not worry about the other things.

One person may take an Asian position, another an Western one, another whatever position he wants; the important thing, I repeat, is to be comfortable so you can have a good meditation. Every person is unique and should look for the most comfortable position without being held by any rule, pattern, or position.

It is very convenient to relax the body. It is indispensable that the chosen position feels good to the body.

Many times I have explained to all of you how to work with the mantra **HAM-SAH**; pronounced *HAM* (silently, with the inhalation), *SAH* (vocalized aloud, exhaling like a soft sigh).[40] This mantra is the wonderful symbol that in Asia makes the chaotic water of life fertile, the symbol of the Third Logos. It is very important to know how to vocalize this mantra and to know about its powers.

Normally sexual forces flow from inside out (centrifugal way); due to that, wet dreams occur when having a dream based on the sexual center.

If someone organized their vital systems and instead of propitiating the centrifugal system used the centripetal system, that means to make the sexual forces run from outside in, making use of transmutation, then even if they had an erotic dream there would be no wet

---

40 Pronounced with A as the ah in "father," M extended as if humming, "mmmmm," S extended like a hiss, "sssss."

dreams. But because people do not have their sexual forces organized, they have wet dreams, the loss of the sacred sperm or spermatic liquor. If we want to avoid wet dreams, we have to learn to organize our sexual forces.

These forces are profoundly related to breath, to Prana, to life; that is obvious.

There is a close and deep relation between sexual forces and respiration. Both, well combined and harmonized, originate profound changes on the anatomy and the psychology of people. What is important is to make the sexual forces run within and upward on a centripetal course. Only in that way is it possible to produce a radical change in the work and functions that can be accomplished by the creative sexual force.

It is necessary to imagine the creative energy in action during meditation. We have to make it rise to the brain in a natural and rhythmic way, using the vocalization of the mantra that I explained before without forgetting the synchronization of the inhalations and exhalations in perfect concentration, harmony, and rhythm.

It is very important to clarify that inhalation should be more profound than exhalation, because that way we make the creative energy flow from outside in. With this practice there is a time when all the creative energy will flow from outside inward and upward.

The creative energy directed each time from outside inward deeper and deeper becomes an extraordinary tool for the Essence to awaken consciousness.

I am teaching the legitimate White Tantra.[41] This is the practice used in the Tantric schools of the Himalayas and Hindustan. This is the way to ecstasy and Samadhi,[42] whatever you wish to call it.

During this practice you should keep your eyes closed without thinking of anything. Unfortunately, some desires may hit the mind; we should study them without identifying with them. After these desires have been understood fully in all their aspects, then we are able to disinte-

---

41 In Asian mysticism, tantra is the class of teachings that was traditionally reserved for the most qualified and serious students. See glossary.

42 In Raja Yoga, Samadhi is the ultimate of the eight steps, in which the practitioner has extracted the consciousness from all conditioning and can thereby experience the reality of any given thing.

grate and destroy them using the spear of Eros.

But if suddenly we remember something that happened to us that brings us rage, what can we do? Stop the rhythmic breathing for a while and try to understand that event which caused that rage in you. Let us study that situation carefully in every detail and disintegrate it with the bistoury [surgical knife] of self-criticism and then forget it and continue our meditation and breathing.

And if suddenly it comes to our mind the memory of a past event of our life that happened ten or twenty years ago, use the same self-criticism and the same bistoury to disintegrate such a memory to discover what truth is to be found there.

Continue the meditation and respiration without thinking, while chanting the mantra **HAM-SAH**, lengthening the inhalation with *HAM* and shortening the exhalation with *SAH*. Repeat the mantra *Hhhhhhaaaaammmmm - Sssssssaaaaaaahhhhhh*, remaining completely calm of mind; only in that way will the Essence be able to escape for a moment in order to submerge herself in reality.

A lot has been said about the
Illuminating Void.[43] We will, of course, be
able to experience it, and in this emptiness we will discover the laws of nature.
We can see these laws not in the way
we normally see them, but the way they
really are. In this physical world we can
see figures from outside, but can we see
them as they really are within, or from the
sides, etc.? In the Illuminating Void we
can know the truth as it really is and not
the way it appears to us. We can experience the truth of an ant, a world, a sun, a
comet, etc.

The Essence submerged in the
Illuminating Void perceives with its spa-
tial sense everything that was, is, and will
be. Her radiations will reach the personality and the mind. It is interesting to know
that while the Essence is submerged in
the Illuminating Void, it experiences reality. The emotional and motor centers will
integrate with the intellectual center, and
the receptive mind will capture the information received by the Essence. For that
reason the information is accumulated
in the intellectual center; thus, we do not
lose it when the Essence comes out of the

43   See glossary.

Illuminating Void and penetrates the personality.

It has been said that to obtain Emptiness we need a suction pump. We have that pump in the spine in the channels Ida and Pingala[44] used by the creative energy to reach the brain. Also it has been said that we need a dynamo; we have one in our brain and willpower. It is obvious that we also need a generator. Fortunately this is the procreative organs (the sexual organs and willpower).

Having the system and elements, we can reach the luminous Emptiness; the pump, the dynamo and the generator are the elements we need to reach the Illuminating Void in our meditations. Only through the Illuminating Void can we know reality, but it is necessary that the Essence penetrates the absolute Emptiness.

In the old texts, they talk a lot about the Holy Okidanokh: Omnipresent, Omnipenetrating, and Omniscient. He comes from the Sacred Absolute Sun. How can we know truly the Holy

---

44 The two channels or serpents on the caduceus of Mercury. Also called Od and Obd, Adam and Eve, Rasana and Lalana, etc.

Okidanokh if we cannot penetrate the luminous Emptiness? It is well known that the Holy Okidanokh is within the Illuminating Void; it is one with the great Emptiness.

When you are in ecstasy, you surpass personality; when you are inside of the luminous Void and experience the reality of the Holy Okidanokh, you are one with the leaves, the water... you live everything that exists. The only thing you need is courage so you do not lose the ecstasy, because when one feels that one is diluted in everything and feels that one is everything, one experiences the fear of annihilation.

One thinks: "Where am I? Why am I everywhere?" Reasoning comes and one can lose the ecstasy returning to the trap again, enclosed again by the personality; but if one has courage, one does not lose his ecstasy.

At this moment, one is like a drop that is submerged in the ocean, but one has to realize that the ocean is submerged in the drop as well. You will feel you are a bird flying, a deep forest, a petal of a flower, the children who play with a butterfly, an elephant, etc. This situation brings terror and you can fail in your meditation.

It is indeed in the Sacred Absolute Sun where one comes to know the final truth. In the Sacred Absolute Sun there is no time. There, the time factor has no existence. There, the universe is all one and the phenomena of nature take place beyond time.

In the Sacred Absolute Sun we can live in an instant eternity. There, one lives beyond good and evil, transformed into radiant creatures.

Therefore, once one has experienced truth, he cannot be like those whose lives are based on creed, no; there, one experiences the urgent necessity of working in the Innermost Self-realization of one's Being here and now.

It is one thing to experience or to truly live the Illuminating Void and another is to achieve Innermost Self-realization. Because of this we need to know how to meditate, to learn to meditate; it is urgent to understand meditation.

I hope that you listeners will understand this, that you will practice meditation so one day you will be able to liberate the Essence and experience the truth for yourselves. The one who is able to liberate the Essence and to enter the Illuminating Void will be distinct; he will no longer be like the others. For this you need a special course; such persons will be different, ready to fight up to the maximum with their only purpose being to realize here and now the Illuminating Void within.

In Asia, when a disciple reaches these marvellous experiences by experiencing the truth and comes to tell his guru, the guru strikes him hard with his hands; it is clear that if the disciple has not ordered his mind, then he will react against the guru. Will he not? However, these disciples are already well trained. Gurus do this to equilibrate the values and to test the disciple, to see how he is progressing in the elimination of his defects.

I hope that all of you have understood deeply what the science of meditation really is; I hope that you will practice intensively in your homes and in places of meditation.

Question: Master, how can we control the fear when we feel that we are in the Illuminating Void?

Samael Aun Weor: It is necessary to fight fear, forcing it to disintegration, until it is converted to cosmic dust. For that reason we have given you specific techniques for disintegrating your defects, using the spear and with the help of your Divine Mother. Of this, we have spoken amply in my book, *The Mystery of the Golden Blossom*.

Chapter 13

Astral Projection

My friends, it is important for you to comprehend the necessity of learning how to leave the physical body at will. I want you to understand that the physical body is a house within which we must not be as prisoners. It is indispensable to enter into the region of the dead at will, to visit the celestial regions, to know other worlds of the infinite space.

Outside of the physical body, one can give to himself the luxury of invoking beloved relatives who already passed through the doors of death. They will concur to our call. Then, we can personally chat with them. There are necromantic magicians who know how to invoke the deceased ones in order to make them visible and tangible in this physical world. Nonetheless, we prefer to visit them in the region where they live in order to know how their situation is, etc.

When out of the physical body, we can acquire complete knowledge about the mysteries of death and life. Out of the physical body, we can invoke the angels in order to talk personally with them face to face.

It is good for you to understand that we had other bodies in the past, we had other existences. When we are out of the physical body, we can remember those existences; we can revive them with complete exactitude.

The clue in order to go out of this dense form, out of this carnal body, is very simple. Attend to me very well, listen: in those instants of transition that exist between vigil and dream one can escape from the body of flesh and bones at will.

A very special case comes into my memory in these moments: Some time ago, I arrived to a town and looked for a hotel, but all the hotels were full; there were no accommodations for anyone. Nonetheless, I obtained accommodation within a hall for guests. There were many beds where the guests were sleeping. I paid for the last one of those beds that was vacant and I fell asleep on it. However, it so happen that at about midnight, a man knocked at the door of that house asking for accommodation. The owner of that business took him to our hall and told him, "I do not have beds, look: all of them are occupied."

The guest complained and said, "There is no accommodation in any place, thus I am determined to sleep in this hall, even though I will do it on the floor. Please, place on the floor for me a floor mat, rug, or carpet and a pillow for my head, because I am very tired."

The lady, the owner of that guest house, was touched, and joyfully consented to what that man asked. I was awake, seeing and hearing everything. Then, the cited guest laid down on the floor, and he intended to fall asleep. I observed details while the man was in the vigil state: he moved from one side to the other as if he wanted to accommodate himself to the hard floor. Then suddenly, he became still and I saw with astonishment an ovoid, grayish cloud that was leaving through the pores of his skin around all his body. The cloud floated for a few instants over that tired body and finally, placing itself in a vertical position, it took the figure of that pilgrim. He fixedly stared at me and thereafter, he walked normally and left the hall.

Behold, my friends: that always happens while in the state of transition between vigil and dream. The pilgrim simply withdrew from his dense form.

All of you do the same thing, but in an unconscious way. I do not want to tell you with this, that the gentleman from this story had performed a conscious astral projection. Nonetheless, the same action can be performed positively and consciously by will.

Indeed, this is a natural process. Therefore, to become aware of our own natural processes can never be dangerous. To consciously perform all of our functions instead of performing them unconsciously and unwillingly, is in no way dangerous. Therefore, I put certain emphasis on the necessity of taking advantage of the instant of transition between vigil and dream, in order to abandon the body of flesh and bones, thus entering into the region of mysteries.

There are incredulous people who say, "What can you know about that which is the beyond? What can you know about that which is from the heaven above? Have you perhaps gone into the other world and come back again?" Etc.

Dear friends, I assure you that with this procedure you can go into the other world and return from it. I can swear to you by what I love the most in life, that I go into the other world each time that it pleases me, and that you can go also. What is important for you is to not be afraid.

When I want to depart from my physical body at will, I take advantage of that instant in which I am slumbering, in that moment in which one is neither completely awake nor completely asleep. Thus, in that precise moment, I perform what that pilgrim of my story performed. I get up very softly, feeling myself as if I were vaporous, fluidic, gaseous, then I leave my room as that mentioned guest from the guest house did, and I direct myself towards the street.

Space is infinite; thus, flying, I can go to any place of the Earth or the infinite. You can do the same, my dear friends. The whole matter rests only on your will to do it.

First of all, you must not identify with the material body. In the precise moment of executing the experiment, you must think that you are not the body; you must comprehend that you are soul. You must feel yourself as being a fluidic, subtle soul. Thereafter, feeling thus, in that state, simply get up from your bed.

What I am stating must be translated as facts, my dear friends. Listen to me very well: it is not a matter of *thinking* that you are getting up from your bed, otherwise, you will remain there thinking that, and you will not perform the experiment. I repeat: what I am emphasizing must be translated into facts. You must perform exactly what that pilgrim of my story performed; he did not position himself to *think* that he was going to depart from his body, he simply acted: he simply got up from the hard floor where he was lying down. I repeat with complete clarity: he got up being subtle, vaporous; thus, like that, he departed from that place.

When are you going to understand me? In which epoch of the history of your lives are you going to learn to depart from your physical body at will?

Do you want to know something from the beyond? Do you want to chat with divine beings face to face? Then, when you are out of your physical body, invoke them, call them with shouts; it is clear that they will concur because of their love towards you, with the purpose of instructing you.

The whole matter that is needed is to abandon laziness and to pay attention to the process of dreaming, because the blankets, bedclothes, or sheets with which one is covered are very pleasant, and it is very difficult to leave the indolence, the slothfulness. Remember that willpower is indispensable; thus, if you exert your will in order to depart from your body, you will achieve it, if you follow my instruction with exactitude.

All of the sages of the past abandoned the dense form in order to consciously and positively travel in infinite space. Then, they spoke with the holy gods. Thus, they received marvelous instructions.

When we are outside of this physical world, we can experience in a direct way all the mysteries of life and death.

Now, you comprehend why I put so much emphasis on the necessity of learning how to depart from the physical body at will.

Question: Master, is it necessary to have some previous learning in order to depart from the physical body, or are there some who know how to do it from birth? I have heard many people say, "I know how to travel in the astral world." Would you explain if this is the same?

Samael Aun Weor: My respected lady, your question is certainly very suitable. In the name of the truth, I have to tell you that nobody had to teach me how to astral project myself, because I was born with that faculty; this is why I know the mysteries of life and death. Now, you can explain to yourself where I get all of the knowledge that I have written in my books. Nonetheless, my case is not an exception: my wife Litelantes also knows how to depart from her physical body at will. We astral travel together: we visit the temples of mysteries, we help many people from remote places, we investigate mysteries, we talk with the gods, the angels, and with the ineffable devas. Thus, when we return into our physical bodies we bring the same memories. This is similar to when two persons leave their homes in order to have some recreation on Sunday, and then they return and talk about the distinct occurrences of their journey.

There are many people in distinct parts of the planet Earth who know how to depart from the physical body at will. Therefore, it is necessary that you also learn how to do it in order for you to know the great marvels of Nature and the cosmos and in order to know what is beyond death.

Question: Master, you tell us that in order to project oneself into the astral plane, one has to take advantage of that given moment when one is between vigil and dream; can we not make it in other moments?

Samael Aun Weor: Dear young lady, I want you to know that when one is very skilful in this matter of astral projection, one can escape from the physical body at will, even if your carnal body is seated or if it is on its feet. However, I repeat, the latter is only for very practical, skillful people. What is normal and natural is to lay down on the bed in order to astral project oneself.

Question: Master, can we invoke any special master for help in our astral projection attempt?

Samael Aun Weor: Friend, allow me to tell you that there are invisible beings who can help. Nonetheless, you can ask for help from your own particular Divine Mother. I am referring to your own Mother Nature, because it is obvious that each one has their own. You must beseech Her in the name of Christ so that she can take you out of your body in the precise instant in which you are in that state of transition between vigil and dream.

Question: Master, is there any special prayer to call our particular Mother Nature? If there is, can you teach it to us?

Samael Aun Weor: Benevolent disciple who is listening to me, I am going to give you advice which can assist anybody in the world: you must lay down on your bed, facing upwards with your body very well relaxed, and become sleepy while reciting with your thought and with your heart the following prayer:

> **"I believe in God,**
> **I believe in my Divine Mother,**

And I believe in white magic;

Mother of mine, take me out of my body."

You must recite this magical prayer with full devotion and with intense faith. Become sleepy, and if it is necessary, you must pray it millions of times. However, remember that saying which states, "Strike with thy rod while thou art begging God."

Thus, when you feel yourself in that state of lassitude which is proper to sleep, when in your mind the first images of dreaming start to appear, then please, I beg you, defeat your laziness, and, feeling yourself like a delicate and subtle phantom, perform what the pilgrim of our story did in the hall of that guest house; that is: get up from your bed and leave your home. Understood?

Question: Master, can we ask our particular Mother Nature to take us to a specific place, or does she takes us where we must go in accordance with our preparation?

Samael Aun Weor: The question you ask is very good. Our Divine Mother knows the place where she can take each one of us. Nonetheless, we also can ask her to take us to this or that given place; thus, if she wants to do it, very well. Nevertheless, if she does not want to take us where we want, but instead she transports us to another place, then we must accept her decision happily, because it is clear that our Mother knows what we need, that which is most convenient to us.

Chapter 14

The Astral Body

Within occultist literature, a great deal has been written regarding this very interesting theme of astral projection.

Here, it is very opportune to cite the undesirable hypnotic phenomena of the mentioned Laurent (July 10, 1894) in which the famous hypnotist Colonel Rochas experimented with hypnotism. He achieved with lamentable imprudence (like those who despise the classic *Ars Magna Brevis Experimentum Periculosum*) what can be summarized as hypnotic states separated from each other by many other lethargic states (people who are dedicated to this subject matter know all this very well).

Onto the three typical hypnotic states known as lethargy, catalepsy, and somnambulism, Colonel Rochas added many other more profound states, thirteen in all. These states were separated from each other by successive lethargic states in which the patient seems to sleep more and more in order to successively awaken into "new states" each time more distant from the state of vigil.

In state number five, a blue phantom appears on the left side of the hypnotized patient. Likewise, in state number six, on the patient's left side another phantom appears but red. Then, upon reaching state number seven, both phantoms unite and become one and when reaching state number eight interpenetrate into irregular white-violet bands.

In state number nine, the astral double, thus integrated, starts to enhance a relative liberty of movements, although without severing the silver cord that connects to the physical body, since the rupture of that cord would signify death.

In hypnotic state number eleven (according to the sayings of Colonel Rochas), the astral double tends to its emancipation, to become totally released from its physical ties, while some certain repugnant forms or diabolic "I's" viciously move in and out of the double, producing terrible convulsions within the patient.

Now that we have reached this section of this chapter, it is convenient to clarify that Colonel Rochas qualified the demonic "I's" of the patient as "repugnant larvae."

When the unhappy patient sees himself assaulted by such animalistic creatures (each time increasing in number), he feels the loss of his vital forces and in anguish asks to be awakened and thus liberated from that nightmare. This is state number twelve.

State number thirteen is definitive: the hypnotized patient is totally released from his physical ties; thus, he freely travels within the superior dimensions of space.

It is clearly comprehendible that all of these hypnotic experiments are criminal in their depth. The hypnotist in this case is similar to a pitiless vivisectionist that, with his bit of intelligence, boasts about being wise and tortures poor animals in order to discover the enigmas of nature. The only difference is that in the hypnotic experiment of our narration, the guinea pig is the unhappy hypnotized patient.

The universal Christian Gnostic Movement teaches practical and effective systems in order to separate the double from the physical body at will, and to consciously travel with the double without harmful and detrimental hypnotic trances.

The wise law of contrary analogies invites us to comprehend that if there are thirteen subjective and negative states during a hypnotic state for the projection of the double, likewise, there are another thirteen objective and positive states during a healthy and natural projection of the double.

It is urgent to comprehend that whosoever wants to learn how to consciously travel within the double, the first thing that he needs to do is to awaken his consciousness.

Astral projection is no longer a problem when the consciousness awakens. Sacred scriptures insist on the necessity of awakening, but people continue with their consciousness asleep.

The time has arrived in which we have to comprehend that the double (which was registered in some photographic films and which was analyzed by the Colonel Rochas) is not the true astral body.

The double has been, is, and shall always be of a molecular, lunar, and protoplasmatic nature.

The astral body is a body of an electronic, solar nature. The astral solar body has nothing vague, vaporous, or subjective. The astral solar body is a body of bones and flesh; it is made out of the flesh from paradise, not from the flesh that comes from Adam.

Ordinary human beings (except those very few rare cases) are always born with the famous lunar double and never with the solar astral body.

The wretched intellectual beast possesses the molecular body, body of desires, or lunar double. He does not have a solar astral body. He must build the solar astral body.

Intellectual animals live inside their physical body; yet, during normal sleep and also after death, they live outside of it. Thus, when outside of their physical bodies, they wander around dressed with their molecular double. Pseudo-esoteric and pseudo-occultist people have named the molecular body "astral body." Nonetheless, that molecular body is not the astral body.

The so-called "incorporeal travels" are always performed with the lunar double; after having released its physical ties, it can freely travel through the whole Milky Way without any danger.

Any monk can develop the superior emotional center, and if he is really self-determined, he can eliminate from his interior nature his lower desires and animal passions. Nevertheless, this is not how one builds the astral body.

This issue related with the building of the astral body has been, is, and shall always be an absolutely sexual problem.

There is an esoteric maxim that states: "As above, so below." We can also state: "As below, so above."

If sexual union of the phallus and the uterus is always necessary in order to engender a physical body, then it is also absolutely logical to state that the sexual act is indispensably necessary in order to engender the solar astral body.

Once in a while within this complicated and difficult labyrinth of pseudo-esotericism and pseudo-occultism, some wandering degenerated infrasexual might appear who will possibly state that the astral body can be built without the necessity of the sexual act because we already have the two poles, masculine and feminine. Those imbecile ignoramuses do not want to comprehend that the time of the Lemurian[45] hermaphrodites[46] has already passed, and that creation without sexual cooperation, without the necessity of the sexual act between man and woman, can only be performed by an authentic hermaphrodite.

The Lemurian hermaphrodites had the phallus and the uterus and also all of the male and female organs totally developed; this is why they could create or reproduce themselves without the necessity of the sexual act. However, all of the pseudo-esoteric and pseudo-occultist people who hate sexual magic[47] have never demonstrated unto us that they have the male and female sexual organs totally developed.

What is as abundant as evil weeds in this perverse, corrupted, and doomed Aryan civilization are the false hermaph-

---

45 The ancient people of the third root race who populated the Earth before the Atlanteans. The division of sexes occured during the Lemurian epoch.
46 From Greek "Hermes-Aphrodite," to indicate a being capable of self-reproduction.
47 See glossary.

rodites, meaning, the homosexuals of Lilith,[48] the gays.

The sexual hydrogen is developed within the human organism according to the musical scale DO-RE-MI-FA-SOL-LA-SI.

The sexual hydrogen SI-12 is very abundant in the semen;[49] this type of hydrogen crystallizes into new human bodies, and when it is wisely transmuted, it takes form within the astral body.

By restraining the sexual impulse in order to avoid the ejaculation of semen, the sexual hydrogen SI-12 receives a special shock that passes it into another second superior octave. This new octave is processed according to the seven notes of the scale DO-RE-MI-FA-SOL-LA-SI.

An esotericist must never ignore that the transformation of substances within the human organism is processed according to the law of the octaves.

The union of the sexual hydrogens SI-12 from a male and female and everything that accompanies these two unities

48 In Kabbalah, Lilith is the mother of demons, the source of many demonic spirits (elementaries) who plague humanity.

49 Semen literally means "seed," which is obviously present in male and female bodies.

allows us to pass the sexual hydrogen into a second, superior octave, whose outcome is the crystallization of the mentioned hydrogen into the marvelous form that is the astral body. That body of perfection is born of the same material, of the same substance, of the same matter from which the physical body is born. Indeed, this is what the transmutation of lead into gold is; in other words, the transmutation of the physical body into the astral body.

Any organism needs its nourishment, and the astral body is no exception. The nourishment of this body of gold is hydrogen 24.

JESUS CALLING US TO AWAKEN.

"Take ye heed, watch and pray: for ye know
not when the time is. For the Son of Man is as
a man taking a far journey, who left his house,
and gave authority to his servants, and to every
man his work, and commanded the porter
to watch. Watch ye therefore: for ye know
not when the master of the house cometh, at
even, or at midnight, or at the cockcrowing,
or in the morning: Lest coming suddenly he
find you sleeping. And what I say unto you
I say unto all, Watch." —Mark 13:33-37

Epilogue

Useless Dreams

Let us now talk about something very important: I want to emphatically address the subject-matter related with dreams. The hour has arrived in which we must delve deeply within this topic.

I acknowledge that the most important thing is to stop dreaming, since indeed, dreams are nothing other than mere projections of the mind and are, therefore, illusions; they are worthless. It is precisely the ego who projects dreams, and obviously those dreams are useless.

We need to transform the subconsciousness into consciousness. We need to radically eliminate not only dreams, but moreover, we must also eliminate the very possibility of dreaming, and this is difficult, since it is unquestionable that such a possibility will always exist so long as subjective elements continue to exist within our psyche.

We need a mind that does not project; we need to exhaust the process of thinking. The projector-mind projects dreams, and they are vain and illusory. When I

talk about the mind as being a projector,
I am not referring merely to "projects,"
such as the ones made by an engineer who
sketches or designs the blueprints for a
building, a bridge, or a road, no; when I
am taking about the mind as a projector, I am addressing the mind of every
intellectual animal. It is clear that the
subconsciousness always projects not only
houses, buildings, or things of the sort;
to be clear, it also projects its memories,
its desires, its emotions, passions, ideas,
experiences, etc. Again, the projector-mind
projects dreams, and it is clear that there
will be projections as long as the subconsciousness continues to exist. When the
subconsciousness ceases to exist, when it
has been transformed into consciousness,
then projections cease, they can no longer
exist; they disappear.

   If we want to attain authentic illumination, then it is necessary and urgent
to transform the subconsciousness into
consciousness. Indubitably, that transformation is only possible by annihilating
the subconsciousness. Yet, the subconsciousness is the ego; so then, we must
annihilate the ego, the "I," the myself, the
self-willed. Yes, this is how the subcon-

sciousness is transformed into consciousness. Consequently, it is necessary for the
subconsciousness to cease to exist, so that
the objective, real, and true consciousness
can appear and occupy its place.

In other words, as long as any subjective element—as insignificant as it might
be—continues to exist within each one
of us, here and now, the possibility of
dreaming will persist; however, when the
subjective elements are terminated, when
not a single subjective element lingers
within our psyche, then the outcome is
objective consciousness, authentic and
true illumination.

Thus, an individual who possesses
objective consciousness, who has eliminated the subconsciousness, lives completely awakened within the supersensible
worlds,[50] and while his physical body
sleeps in the bed, he will move in those
worlds willingly: seeing, hearing, and per-
ceiving the great realities of the superior
worlds.

Therefore, it is one thing to go about
within the hypersensible worlds with
objective consciousness, in other words,

---

50 The worlds that exist beyond the reach of the
physical senses: from Latin super, "beyond."

with awakened consciousness, and it is another to do so in a subjective or sub-conscious state, in other words, by going around projecting dreams.

Lo and behold the great difference between the one who goes around project-ing dreams within those hypersensible regions, and the one who lives there without making any projections, who has the consciousness completely awakened, illuminated, in a state of a super-exalted vigilance. Obviously, the latter is truly an enlightened one, and can (if one wishes) investigate the mysteries of life and death and know all of the enigmas of the uni-verse.

A certain author states somewhere that dreams are nothing other than disguised ideas, and if this statement is factual, we then can clarify this matter a little more by stating that "dreams are projections of the mind" and therefore, are false and vain; thus, whosoever lives awakened no longer dreams.

Without having died within them-selves, without having annihilated the ego, the "I", the myself, no one can live awakened; this is why I want all of you brothers and sisters to occupy yourselves with the disintegration of your egos, because only thus, by disintegrating your terrible legion, can you be radically awakened.

Indubitably, to eliminate our subjective elements is not easy, since they are many and widely varied. This elimination is processed in a didactical way, little by little. Therefore, accordingly, as one is eliminating such elements, one is objectifying one's consciousness. Thus, when elimination has become absolute, then the consciousness has become totally objectified, awakened; then the possibility of dreaming has been terminated, concluded.

The great adepts of the Universal White Fraternity do not dream, since they possess objective consciousness; for them the possibility of dreaming has disappeared. Thus, one finds them within the superior worlds in a state of intensified vigilance, totally illuminated, and directing the current of the innumerable centuries, governing the laws of nature, converted into gods who are beyond good and evil.

It is therefore indispensable to comprehend this matter in depth. Thus, in order for all of you to have an exact summary of this, I want to tell you the following:

1. The subconsciousness is the ego; thus, annihilate the ego and the consciousness will awaken.

2. The subconscious elements are infrahuman elements that every one of us carries within, therefore destroy them and the possibility of dreaming will cease.

3. Dreams are projections of the ego and therefore they are worthless.

4. The ego is mind.

5. Dreams are projections of the mind.

6. You must mark down the following with much attention: It is indispensable to stop projecting.

7. We must not only stop projecting things of the future, but of the past, since we live constantly projecting things from yesterday.

8. We must also stop projecting every type of present emotions, morbidities, passions, etc.

The projections of the mind are therefore infinite; as a consequence, the possibilities of dreaming are infinite. Therefore, how can a dreamer be considered an illuminated one? Obviously, the dreamer is nothing other than a dreamer who does not know anything about the reality of things, about that which is beyond the world of dreams.

It is indispensable that our brothers and sisters of the Gnostic Movement concern themselves with their awakening. For this, it is required that they truly dedicate themselves to the dissolution of their "I," their ego, their myself, their self-willed; may that be their main preoccupation. Accordingly, as they are dying within themselves, their consciousness will become successively more and more objective; thus, the possibilities of dreaming will diminish in a progressive way.

It is indispensable to meditate in order to comprehend our psychological errors. When one comprehends that one has this or that defect or error, one can give oneself the luxury of eliminating it, as I taught in my book *The Mystery of the Golden Blossom*.

To eliminate this or that error, this or that psychological defect, is equivalent to eliminating this or that psychological aggregate, this or that subjective element, within which subsists the possibilities of dreaming or projecting dreams.

When we want to eliminate a defect, an error or a psychic aggregate, we must first of all comprehend it; nonetheless, brothers and sisters, it is not enough to only comprehend, it is necessary to delve even deeper, to be more profound: it is necessary to "capture" the deep significance of that which one has comprehended, and one can only achieve such a "capture" by means of a very internal, in-depth, profound meditation...

The one who has captured the deep significance of that which has been comprehended has the possibility of eliminating it. To eliminate psychic aggregates is urgent. Psychic aggregates and psychological defects are basically the same; thus any psychic aggregate is nothing else than the expression of a type of psychological defect...

That there is the need to eliminate them, this is clear. However, we must first of all comprehend them and also to have captured their deep significance. Thus, this is how we die from moment to moment; the new comes to us only with death.

Many want to be awakened in the astral, mental, etc., planes, yet they do not preoccupy themselves with psychological death, and what is worse is that they confuse their dreams with true mystical experiences. Dreams, which are nothing other that simple projections of the subconsciousness, are one thing, yet real mystical experiences are another thing. Any authentic mystical experience demands the state of alertness and awakened consciousness. I cannot conceive of mystical experiences with sleeping consciousness. Therefore, the mystical, real, and authentic experience only arrives when the objectiveness of the consciousness has been achieved, when we are awakened.

May all our brothers and sisters profoundly reflect upon all of this. Study our book *The Mystery of the Golden Blossom*. May everyone preoccupy themselves with dying from moment to moment. Only in this way can they achieve the total objectiveness of their consciousness.

Question: Master, are all of those crowds who go everywhere running like mad people asleep? Are they going around projecting? Are they dreaming? Are they alienated to themselves?

Samael Aun Weor: Indeed, those people who go everywhere in a mad rush, running, they are dreaming. It is not necessary for their physical bodies to be resting, snoring in their beds at midnight, in order for them to be dreaming. People dream right here in flesh and bone, just as you see them, running as mad people in the street, as they go around in this constant coming and going, like machines without rhyme or reason, nor any orientation. Thus, in the same way they go around within the internal worlds when their physical body sleeps in their bed.

Regrettably, what happens is that people who are daydreaming in their life, that go around dreaming in their wrongly called "state of vigil" (since, in that state, one always see them sleeping, dreaming), when the hour in which their physical bodies must rest in their bed arrives, they abandon their physical vehicle and penetrate within the supersensible worlds;

however, they carry their dreams to such regions. In other words, each one carries their dreams to the internal worlds, as much as during the hours in which the physical body is sleeping, as well as after their physical death.

Indeed, people die without knowing how, and, dreaming, they enter into the internal worlds and there they live, dreaming; thereafter, they are born without knowing at what time or how, and continue going around dreaming in their practical life constantly.

Therefore, it is not strange that people accidentally die under the wheels of cars, that they commit so much madness, since this happens because they have their consciousness asleep, since they are dreaming...

It is indispensable to cease dreaming. The one who ceases dreaming here and now also ceases dreaming in any corner of the universe and can then go everywhere awakened. The one who awakens here and now awakens in the infinite, in the superior worlds, in any place of the cosmos.

What is important is to awaken here and now, in this very moment in which we are talking, to awaken from instant to instant, from moment to moment.

Glossary

Absolute: Abstract space; that which is without attributes or limitations. The Absolute has three aspects: the Ain, the Ain Soph, and the Ain Soph Aur.

"The Absolute is the Being of all Beings. The Absolute is that which Is, which always has Been, and which always will Be. The Absolute is expressed as Absolute Abstract Movement and Repose. The Absolute is the cause of Spirit and of Matter, but It is neither Spirit nor Matter. The Absolute is beyond the mind; the mind cannot understand It. Therefore, we have to intuitively understand Its nature." —Samael Aun Weor, *Tarot and Kabbalah*

"In the Absolute we go beyond karma and the gods, beyond the law. The mind and the individual consciousness are only good for mortifying our lives. In the Absolute we do not have an individual mind or individual consciousness; there, we are the unconditioned, free and absolutely happy Being. The Absolute is life free in its movement, without conditions, limitless, without the mortifying fear of the law, life beyond spirit and matter, beyond karma and suffering, beyond thought, word and action, beyond silence and sound, beyond forms." — Samael Aun Weor, *The Major Mysteries*

Astral: This term is derived from "pertaining to or proceeding from the stars," but in the esoteric knowledge it refers to the emotional aspect of the fifth dimension, which in Hebrew is called Hod.

Astral Body: What is commonly called the astral body is not the true astral body, it is rather the lunar protoplasmatic body, also known as the kama rupa (Sanskrit, "body of desires") or "dream body" (Tibetan rmi-lam-gyi lus). The true astral body is solar (being superior to lunar nature) and must be created, as the Master Jesus indicated in the Gospel of John 3:5-6, "Except a man be born of water and of the Spirit, he cannot enter into the kingdom of God. That which is born of the flesh is flesh; and that which is born of the Spirit is spirit." The solar astral body is created as a result of the Third Initiation of Major Mysteries (Serpents of Fire), and is perfected in the Third Serpent of Light. In Tibetan Buddhism, the solar astral body is known as the illusory body (sgyu-lus). This body is related to the emotional center and to the sephirah Hod.

"Really, only those who have worked with the Maithuna (White Tantra) for many years can possess the astral body." —Samael Aun Weor, *The Elimination of Satan's Tail*

Being: Our inner, divine Source, also called the Innermost or Monad, which is not easily definable in conceptual terms. The use of the term "Being" is important though, in relation to its roots:

From the Online Etymology Dictionary: "beon, beom, bion "be, exist, come to be, become," from beo-, beu-, from base bheu-, bhu- "grow, come into being, become." It also is related to the Sanskrit bhavah "becoming," bhavati "becomes, happens," bhumih "earth, world."

"The conception we have of the Being is not the Being. Any intellectual concept we have created about the Being is not the Being. Our opinion of the Being is not the Being. The Being is the Being, and the reason for the Being to be is to be itself." —Samael Aun Weor, *The Secret Doctrine of Anahuac*

Buddhata: Derived from "buddhadatu or buddhadhatu" (Sanskrit), which means "essence of the Buddha," (from dhatu, "element, primary element, cause, mineral"). The term buddhadhatu appeared in Mahayana scripture as a reference to tathagatagarbha, the "embryo of the Buddha," also called Buddha Nature. In general use, this describes that element in us that has the potential to become a Buddha, an "awakened one."

Centers, Seven: The human being has seven centers of psychological activity. The first five are the intellectual, emotional, motor, instinctive, and sexual centers. However, through inner development one learns how to utilize the superior emotional and superior intellectual centers. Most people do not use these two at all.

Chakra: (Sanskrit) Literally, "wheel." The chakras are subtle centers of energetic transformation. There are hundreds of chakras in our hidden physiology, but seven primary ones related to the awakening of consciousness.

"The Chakras are centres of Shakti as vital force... The Chakras are not perceptible to the gross senses. Even if they were perceptible in the living body which they help to organise, they disappear with the disintegration of organism at death." —Swami Sivananda, *Kundalini Yoga*

"The chakras are points of connection through which the divine energy circulates from one to another vehicle of the human being." —Samael Aun Weor, *Aztec Christic Magic*

Consciousness: "Wherever there is life, there exists the consciousness. Consciousness is inherent to life as humidity is inherent to water." —Samael Aun Weor, *Fundamental Notions of Endocrinology and Criminology*

From various dictionaries: 1. The state of being conscious; knowledge of one's own existence, condition, sensations, mental operations, acts, etc. 2. Immediate knowledge or perception of the presence of any object, state, or sensation. 3. An alert cognitive state in which you are aware of yourself and your situation. In Universal Gnosticism, the range of potential consciousness is allegorized in the Ladder of Jacob, upon which the angels ascend and descend. Thus there are higher and lower levels of consciousness, from the level of demons at the bottom, to highly realized angels in the heights.

"It is vital to understand and develop the conviction that consciousness has the potential to increase to an infinite degree." —The 14th Dalai Lama.

"Light and consciousness are two phenomena of the same thing; to a lesser degree of consciousness, corresponds a lesser degree of light; to a greater degree of consciousness, a greater degree of light." —Samael Aun Weor, *The Esoteric Treatise of Hermetic Astrology*

Divine Mother: The Divine Mother is the eternal, feminine principle, which is formless, and further unfolds into many levels, aspects, and manifestations.

"Devi or Sakti is the Mother of Nature. She
is Nature Itself. The whole world is Her body.
Mountains are Her bones. Rivers are Her veins.
Ocean is Her bladder. Sun, moon are Her eyes.
Wind is Her breath. Agni is Her mouth. She runs
this world show. Sakti is symbolically female;
but It is, in reality, neither male nor female. It
is only a Force which manifests Itself in various
forms. The five elements and their combinations
are the external manifestations of the Mother.
Intelligence, discrimination, psychic power, and
will are Her internal manifestations." —Swami
Sivananda

"Among the Aztecs, she was known as
Tonantzin, among the Greeks as chaste Diana.
In Egypt she was Isis, the Divine Mother, whose
veil no mortal has lifted. There is no doubt at
all that esoteric Christianity has never forsaken
the worship of the Divine Mother Kundalini.
Obviously she is Marah, or better said, RAM-IO,
MARY. What orthodox religions did not specify,
at least with regard to the exoteric or public
circle, is the aspect of Isis in her individual human form. Clearly, it was taught only in secret
to the Initiates that this Divine Mother exists
individually within each human being. It cannot
be emphasized enough that Mother-God, Rhea,
Cybele, Adonia, or whatever we wish to call her,
is a variant of our own individual Being in the
here and now. Stated explicitly, each of us has
our own particular, individual Divine Mother."
—Samael Aun Weor, *The Great Rebellion*

"Devi Kundalini, the Consecrated Queen of
Shiva, our personal Divine Cosmic Individual
Mother, assumes five transcendental mystic as-

pects in every creature, which we must enumerate:

1. The unmanifested Prakriti

2. The chaste Diana, Isis, Tonantzin, Maria or better said Ram-Io

3. The terrible Hecate, Persephone, Coatlicue, queen of the infernos and death; terror of love and law

4. The special individual Mother Nature, creator and architect of our physical organism

5. The Elemental Enchantress to whom we owe every vital impulse, every instinct." —Samael Aun Weor, *The Mystery of the Golden Blossom*

Ego: The multiplicity of contradictory psychological elements that we have inside are in their sum the "ego." Each one is also called "an ego" or an "I." Every ego is a psychological defect which produces suffering. The ego is three (related to our Three Brains or three centers of psychological processing), seven (capital sins), and legion (in their infinite variations).

"The ego is the root of ignorance and pain." —Samael Aun Weor, *The Esoteric Treatise of Hermetic Astrology*

"The Being and the ego are incompatible. The Being and the ego are like water and oil. They can never be mixed... The annihilation of the psychic aggregates (egos) can be made possible only by radically comprehending our errors through meditation and by the evident Self-reflection of the Being." —Samael Aun Weor, *The Gnostic Bible: The Pistis Sophia Unveiled*

Elementaries: "...when Cain had killed Abel, Adam
separated from his wife and cohabited with
two female elementals, and from his intercourse
with them was begotten a great and numerous
progeny of demons and elementaries who at
night time appear in attractive forms and thus
give rise to offspring like unto themselves. In
scripture, they are termed 'the plagues of the
children of men... Woe unto those who are ignorant and therefore unable to avert and ward off
the influence of these defiling elemental beings
that swarm in their myriads throughout the
world. If it were permitted to behold them, we
should be amazed and confounded and wonder
how the world could continue to exist. Observe
that Naamah being the exciter of human con-
cupiscence and carnality, it is obligatory on everyone to practice and perform acts and rites of
purification, so that he may become and preserve
himself pure and undefiled." —Zohar

"Incubi and succubi are formed from the sperm
of those who perform the imaginative anti-
natural act of masturbation (in thoughts or
desires). And because it comes only from the
imagination, it is not genuine sperm (material)
but corrupt salt. Only semen that comes from an
organ selected by Nature for its development can
germinate in a body. When sperm does not come
from appropriate matter (nutritious substratum)
it will not produce anything good, but will generate something useless. For this reason, incubi
and succubi that originate from corrupt semen
are harmful and useless in accordance with the
natural order of things. These germs which are
formed in the imagination are born of Amore

Heress, which signifies the type of love whereby a man imagines a woman, or vice-versa, in order to copulate with the image created within the sphere of his mind. The expulsion of a useless, ethereal fluid results from this act, incapable of producing offspring but instead bringing larvae into existence. Imagination used in this way gives birth to an exuberant shamelessness which, if pursued, can make a man impotent and a woman sterile, because during the frequent practice of any such unhealthy visualization, much real creative energy is lost. The larvae-egos of lasciviousness are real, thinking, autonomous entities within which a good percentage of Consciousness is imprisoned." —Paracelsus, *De Origine Morborum Invisibilium*

"The terms incubus and succubus have been applied indiscriminately by the Church Fathers to elementals. The incubus and succubus, however, are evil and unnatural creations, whereas elementals is a collective term for all the inhabitants of the four elemental essences. According to Paracelsus, the incubus and succubus (which are male and female respectively) are parasitical creatures subsisting upon the evil thoughts and emotions of the Astral body. These terms are also applied to the superphysical organisms of sorcerers and black magicians. While these larvæ are in no sense imaginary beings, they are, nevertheless, the offspring of the imagination. By the ancient sages they were recognized as the invisible cause of vice because they hover in the ethers surrounding the morally weak and continually incite them to excesses of a degrading nature. For this reason they frequent the atmosphere of the dope den, the dive, and the brothel, where they attach themselves to those unfortunates who have given themselves up to iniquity. By permitting his senses to become deadened through indulgence in habit-forming drugs or alcoholic stimulants, the individual becomes temporarily en rapport with these denizens of the astral plane. The houris seen by the hasheesh or opium addict and the lurid monsters which torment the victim of delirium tremens are examples of submundane beings, visible only to those whose evil practices are the magnet for their attraction." — *Secret Teachings of All Ages* (1928) by Manly P. Hall

Fornication: Originally, the term fornication was derived from the Indo-European word gwher, whose meanings relate to heat and burning. Fornication means to make the heat (solar fire) of the seed (sexual power) leave the body through voluntary orgasm. Any voluntary orgasm is fornication, whether between a married man and woman, or an unmarried man and woman, or through masturbation, or in any other case; this is explained by Moses: "A man from whom there is a discharge of semen, shall immerse all his flesh in water, and he shall remain unclean until evening. And any garment or any leather [object] which has semen on it, shall be immersed in water, and shall remain unclean until evening. A woman with whom a man cohabits, whereby there was [a discharge of] semen, they shall immerse in water, and they shall remain unclean until evening." —Leviticus 15:16-18

To fornicate is to spill the sexual energy through the orgasm. Those who "deny themselves" restrain the sexual energy, and "walk in the midst of the fire" without being burned. Those who restrain the sexual energy, who renounce the orgasm, remember God in themselves, and do not defile themselves with animal passion, "for the temple of God is holy, which temple ye are."

"Whosoever is born of God doth not commit sin; for his seed remaineth in him: and he cannot sin, because he is born of God." —1 John 3:9

This is why neophytes always took a vow of sexual abstention, so that they could prepare themselves for marriage, in which they would have sexual relations but not release the sexual energy through the orgasm. This is why Paul advised:

"...they that have wives be as though they had none..." —I Corinthians 7:29

"A fornicator is an individual who has intensely accustomed his genital organs to copulate (with orgasm). Yet, if the same individual changes his custom of copulation to the custom of no copulation, then he transforms himself into a chaste person. We have as an example the astonishing case of Mary Magdalene, who was a famous prostitute. Mary Magdalene became the famous Saint Mary Magdalene, the repented prostitute. Mary Magdalene became the chaste disciple of Christ." —Samael Aun Weor, *The Revolution of Beelzebub*

Gnosis: (Greek) Knowledge.

1. The word Gnosis refers to the knowledge we acquire through our own experience, as opposed to knowledge that we are told or believe in. Gnosis - by whatever name in history or culture - is conscious, experiential knowledge, not merely

intellectual or conceptual knowledge, belief, or theory. This term is synonymous with the Hebrew "daath" and the Sanskrit "jna."

2. The tradition that embodies the core wisdom or knowledge of humanity.

"Gnosis is the flame from which all religions sprouted, because in its depth Gnosis is religion. The word "religion" comes from the Latin word "religare," which implies "to link the Soul to God"; so Gnosis is the very pure flame from where all religions sprout, because Gnosis is Knowledge, Gnosis is Wisdom." —Samael Aun Weor, *The Esoteric Path*

"The secret science of the Sufis and of the Whirling Dervishes is within Gnosis. The secret doctrine of Buddhism and of Taoism is within Gnosis. The sacred magic of the Nordics is within Gnosis. The wisdom of Hermes, Buddha, Confucius, Mohammed and Quetzalcoatl, etc., etc., is within Gnosis. Gnosis is the Doctrine of Christ." —Samael Aun Weor, *The Revolution of Beelzebub*

Human: Although the words human or human being are used generally to refer to the people of this planet, the real meaning of the word human is far more demanding. Human is derived from Latin humanus "of man, human," also "humane, philanthropic, kind, gentle, polite; learned, refined, civilized." In classical philosophy, we are not yet human beings, but have the potential to become so. A famous illustration of this is the story of Diogenes wandering around crowded Athens during this day with an illuminated lantern, searching for "anthropos" (a real human being), yet failing to find even one.

In general, there are three types of human beings:

1. The ordinary person (called human being out of respect), more accurately called the "intellectual animal."

2. The true human being or man (from Sanskrit manas, mind): someone who has created the soul (the solar bodies), symbolized as the chariot of Ezekiel or Krishna, the Wedding Garment of Jesus, the sacred weapons of the heroes of mythology, etc. Such persons are saints, masters, or buddhas of various levels.

3. The superhuman: a true human being who has also incarnated the Cosmic Christ, thus going beyond mere sainthood or buddhahood, and into the highest reaches of liberation. These are the founders of religions, the destroyers of dogmas and traditions, the great rebels of spiritual light.

According to Gnostic anthropology, a true human being is an individual who has conquered the animal nature within and has thus created the soul, the Mercabah of the Kabbalists, the Sahu of the Egyptians, the To Soma Heliakon of the Greeks: this is "the Body of Gold of the Solar Man." A true human being is one with the Monad, the Inner Spirit. It can be said that the true human being or man is the inner Spirit (in Kabbalah, Chesed. In Hinduism, Atman).

"Every spirit is called man, which means that only the aspect of the light of the spirit that

is enclothed within the body is called man. So
the body of the spirit of the holy side is only a
covering; in other words, the spirit is the actual
essence of man and the body is only its covering.
But on the other side, the opposite applies. This
is why it is written: "you have clothed me with
skin and flesh..." (Iyov 10:11). The flesh of man
is only a garment covering the essence of man,
which is the spirit. Everywhere it is written the
flesh of man, it hints that the essence of man
is inside. The flesh is only a vestment for man,
a body for him, but the essence of man is the
aspect of his spirit." —Zohar 1A:10:120

A true human being has reconquered the in-
nocence and perfection of Eden, and has become
what Adam was intended to be: a king or queen
of nature, having power over nature. The intellectual animal, however, is controlled by nature,
and thus is not a true human being. Examples of
true human beings are all those great saints of
all ages and cultures: Jesus, Moses, Mohammed,
Krishna, and many others whose names were
never known by the public.

Hydrogen: (From *hydro-* water, *gen-* generate, genes,
genesis, etc.) The hydrogen is the simplest element on the periodic table and in Gnosticism it
is recognized as the element that is the building block of all forms of matter. Hydrogen is a
packet of solar light. The solar light (the light
that comes from the sun) is the reflection of the
Okidanokh, the Cosmic Christ, which creates
and sustains every world. This element is the
fecundated water, generated water (hydro). The
water is the source of all life. Everything that we
eat, breathe and all of the impressions that we

receive are in the form of various structures of hydrogen. Samael Aun Weor often will place a note (Do, Re, Mi…) and a number related with the vibration and atomic weight (level of complexity) with a particular hydrogen. For example, Samael Aun Weor constantly refers to the Hydrogen Si-12. "Si" is the highest note in the octave and it is the result of the notes that come before it. This particular hydrogen is always related to the forces of Yesod, which is the synthesis and coagulation of all food, air and impressions that we have previously received. Food begins at Do-768, air begins at Do-384, and impressions begin at Do-48.

Illuminating Void: Also called the Absolute, Emptiness, Sunyata.

The ultimate nature of reality, which is impossible to convey in words. In Buddhist philosophy, it is described as paramarthasatya (ultimate truth), dharmata (actual reality), and tathata (suchness), each of which attempt to communicate the total absence of self-identity ("I") and inherent existence. Only through the experience of the voidness or emptiness can one understand it, and that experience can only be reached through a very specific type of meditation.

"Transcendent wisdom is inexpressible and inconceivable. Unborn and unceasing, it has the nature of space; It is realized through an individual's discernment and is the object of pristine awareness. It is the mother of all Buddhas throughout the three periods of time." —Buddha Shakyamuni

"Buddhist Enlightenment is not gained through holding onto or inflating one's self-awareness. On the contrary, it is gained through killing or crushing any attachment to this illuminating consciousness; only by transcending it may one come to the innermost core of Mind—the perfectly free and thoroughly nonsubstantial illuminating-Voidness. This illuminating-Void character, empty yet dynamic, is the Essence (Chinese: ti) of the mind. The important point here is that when the word "Essence" is mentioned, people immediately think of something quintessentially concrete; and when the word "Void" is mentioned, they automatically envision a dead and static "nothingness." Both of these conceptions miss the meanings of the Chinese word ti (Essence) and the Sanskrit word Sunyata (Voidness), and expose the limitation of the finite and one-sided way of human thinking. The ordinary way of thinking is to accept the idea that something is existent or nonexistent, but never that it is both existent and nonexistent at the same time. A is A or not A; but never is it both A and not A simultaneously. In the same way, the verdict of common sense on Voidness versus existence is: "Voidness is not existence, nor is existence Voidness." This pattern of reasoning, regarded as the correct and rational way of thinking, is advocated by logicians as a sine qua non and is accepted by common sense for all practical purposes. But Buddhism does not invariably follow this sine qua non, especially when it deals with the truth of Sunyata. It says: "Form does not differ from Voidness, and Voidness does not differ from Form; Form is

Voidness and Voidness is Form." Buddhism also says that it is owing to Voidness that things can exist and, because of the very fact that things do exist, they must be Void. It emphasizes that Voidness and existence are complementary to each other and not in opposition to each other; they include and embrace, rather than exclude or negate each other. When ordinary sentient beings see an object, they see only its existent, not its void, aspect. But an enlightened being sees both aspects at the same time. This nondistinguishment, or "unification" as some people like to call it, of Voidness and existence, is the so-called Nonabiding Middle Way Doctrine of Mahayana Buddhism. Therefore, Voidness, as understood in Buddhism, is not something negative, nor does it mean absence or extinction. Voidness is simply a term denoting the nonsubstantial and nonself nature of beings, and a pointer indicating the state of absolute nonattachment and freedom. Voidness is not easily explained. It is not definable or describable. As Zen Master Huai Jang has said, "Anything that I say will miss the point." —Garma C.C. Chang, *The Practice of Zen* (1959)

"Only in the absence of the ego can we directly experience Illuminating Emptiness." —Samael Aun Weor, *The Mystery of the Golden Blossom*

"Those who are ignorant of the void cannot achieve liberation. These confused minds wander in the prison of the six realms." —*Bodhichittavivarana*

Infrasexual: From infra, "below, underneath, beneath; later than, smaller, inferior to," from *ndher "under." As opposed to "supra."

Sexuality has three basic levels:

1. Suprasexuality: sexual transmutation to create the soul and the perfect human being. Christ, Buddha, Dante, Zoroaster, Mohammed, Hermes, Quetzalcoatl, and many other great masters were suprasexual.

2. Normal sexuality: sexuality for procreation and the continuity of the species.

3. Infrasexuality: sexuality of the underworld, hell, the abyss, which has now infected humanity worldwide. The degeneration in the use or function of the sexual organs or energy. This includes all forms of sexual perversion, such as sexual violence, sex as power or addiction, pornography, prostitution, masturbation, homosexuality, hatred of sex (such as among religious people), etc.

"It is obvious that the infernal worlds [hell realms] are infrasexual. It is evident that infrasexuality reigns with sovereignty within humanity." —Samael Aun Weor, *Tarot and Kabbalah*

Initiation: The process whereby the Innermost (the Inner Father) receives recognition, empowerment and greater responsibilities in the Internal Worlds, and little by little approaches His goal: complete Self-realization, or in other words, the return into the Absolute. Initiation NEVER applies to the "I" or our terrestrial personality.

"Nine Initiations of Minor Mysteries and seven great Initiations of Major Mysteries exist. The INNERMOST is the one who receives all of these Initiations. The Testament of Wisdom says: "Before the dawning of the false aurora upon the earth, the ones who survived the hurricane and the tempest were praising the INNERMOST, and

the heralds of the aurora appeared unto them."
The psychological "I" does not receives Initiations. The human personality does not receive
anything. Nonetheless, the "I" of some Initiates
becomes filled with pride when saying 'I am a
Master, I have such Initiations.' Thus, this is
how the "I" believes itself to be an Initiate and
keeps reincarnating in order to "perfect itself",
but, the "I" never ever perfects itself. The "I" only
reincarnates in order to satisfy desires. That is
all." —Samael Aun Weor, *The Aquarian Message*

Intellectual Animal: The current state of humanity: animals with intellect.

When the intelligent principle, the Monad,
sends its spark of consciousness into Nature,
that spark, the anima, enters into manifestation
as a simple mineral. Gradually, over millions of
years, the anima gathers experience and evolves
up the chain of life until it perfects itself in the
level of the mineral kingdom. It then graduates
into the plant kingdom, and subsequently into
the animal kingdom. With each ascension the
spark receives new capacities and higher grades
of complexity. In the animal kingdom it learns
procreation by ejaculation. When that animal
intelligence enters into the human kingdom, it
receives a new capacity: reasoning, the intellect;
it is now an anima with intellect: an intellectual
animal. That spark must then perfect itself in the
human kingdom in order to become a complete
and perfect human being, an entity that has conquered and transcended everything that belongs
to the lower kingdoms. Unfortunately, very few
intellectual animals perfect themselves; most
remain enslaved by their animal nature, and thus

are reabsorbed by Nature, a process belonging to the devolving side of life and called by all the great religions "Hell" or the Second Death.

"The present manlike being is not yet human; he is merely an intellectual animal. It is a very grave error to call the legion of the "I" the "soul." In fact, what the manlike being has is the psychic material, the material for the soul within his Essence, but indeed, he does not have a Soul yet." —Samael Aun Weor, *The Revolution of the Dialectic*

"Whosoever possesses the physical, astral, mental, and causal bodies receives the animistic and spiritual principles, and becomes a true human being. Before having them, one is an intellectual animal falsely called a human being. Regarding the face and shape of the physical body of any intellectual animal, they look like the physical characteristics of a human being, however, if their psychological processes are observed and compared with the psychological processes of a human being, then we find that they are completely different, totally distinct." —Samael Aun Weor, *Kabbalah of the Mayan Mysteries*

Internal Worlds: The many dimensions that are more subtle than the physical world, which is why they are called "internal," since they are "within" physicality. All dimensions are here and now, interpenetrating.

There are subjective (projected, illusory worlds) and objective worlds (real, authentic). To know the objective internal worlds (such as the Astral Plane, or Nirvana, or the Klipoth) one must first know and discriminate one's own personal, subjective internal worlds, because the two are intimately associated.

"Whosoever truly wants to know the internal worlds of the planet Earth or of the solar system or of the galaxy in which we live, must previously know his intimate world, his individual, internal life, his own internal worlds. Man, know thyself, and thou wilt know the universe and its gods. The more we explore this internal world called "myself," the more we will comprehend that we simultaneously live in two worlds, in two realities, in two confines: the external and the internal. In the same way that it is indispensable for one to learn how to walk in the external world so as not to fall down into a precipice, or not get lost in the streets of the city, or to select one's friends, or not associate with the perverse ones, or not eat poison, etc.; likewise, through the psychological work upon oneself we learn how to walk in the internal world, which is explorable only through self-observation." —Samael Aun Weor, *Treatise of Revolutionary Psychology*

Through self-observation, we develop the capacity to awaken where previously we were asleep: including in the objective internal worlds.

The internal worlds are mapped on the Tree of Life of Kabbalah.

Kabbalah: (Hebrew קבלה) Alternatively spelled Cabala, Qabalah from the Hebrew קבל KBLH or QBL, "to receive." An ancient esoteric teaching hidden from the uninitiated, whose branches and many forms have reached throughout the world. The true Kabbalah is the science and language of the superior worlds and is thus objective, complete and without flaw; it is said that "All enlightened beings agree," and their natural agreement is a function of the awakened consciousness. The Kabbalah is the language of that consciousness, thus disagreement regarding its meaning and interpretation is always due to the subjective elements in the psyche.

"The objective of studying the Kabbalah is to be skilled for work in the internal worlds... One that does not comprehend remains confused in the internal worlds. Kabbalah is the basis in order to understand the language of these worlds." — Samael Aun Weor, *Tarot and Kabbalah*

"In Kabbalah we have to constantly look at the Hebrew letters." —Samael Aun Weor, *Tarot and Kabbalah*

Kundalini: "Kundalini, the serpent power or mystic fire, is the primordial energy or Sakti that lies dormant or sleeping in the Muladhara Chakra, the centre of the body. It is called the serpentine or annular power on account of serpentine form. It is an electric fiery occult power, the great pristine force which underlies all organic and inorganic matter. Kundalini is the cosmic power in individual bodies. It is not a material force like electricity, magnetism, centripetal or centrifugal force. It is a spiritual potential Sakti or cosmic power. In reality it has no form. [...] O Divine Mother Kundalini, the Divine Cosmic Energy that is hidden in men! Thou art Kali, Durga, Adisakti, Rajarajeswari, Tripurasundari, Maha-Lakshmi, Maha-Sarasvati! Thou hast put on all these names and forms. Thou hast manifested as Prana, electricity, force, magnetism, cohesion, gravitation in this universe. This whole universe rests in Thy bosom. Crores of salutations unto thee. O Mother of this world! Lead me on to open the Sushumna Nadi and take Thee along the Chakras to Sahasrara Chakra and to merge myself in Thee and Thy consort, Lord Siva. Kundalini Yoga is that Yoga which treats of Kundalini Sakti, the six centres of spiritual energy (Shat Chakras), the arousing of the sleeping Kundalini Sakti and its union with Lord Siva in Sahasrara Chakra, at the crown of the head. This is an exact science. This is also known as Laya Yoga. The six centres are pierced (Chakra Bheda) by the passing of Kundalini Sakti to the top of the head. 'Kundala' means 'coiled'. Her form is like a coiled serpent. Hence the name Kundalini." —Swami Sivananda, *Kundalini Yoga*

"The ascent of the Kundalini along the spinal cord is achieved very slowly in accordance with the merits of the heart. The fires of the heart control the miraculous development of the sacred serpent. Devi Kundalini is not something mechanical as many suppose; the igneous serpent is only awakened with genuine love between husband and wife, and it will never rise up along the medullar canal of adulterers."- Samael Aun Weor, *The Mystery of the Golden Blossom*

"The decisive factor in the progress, development and evolution of the Kundalini is ethics." - Samael Aun Weor, *The Revolution of Beelzebub*

"Until not too long ago, the majority of spiritualists believed that on awakening the Kundalini, the latter instantaneously rose to the head and the initiate was automatically united with his Innermost or Internal God, instantly, and converted into Mahatma. How comfortable! How comfortably all these theosophists, Rosicrucians and spiritualists, etc., imagined High Initiation." - Samael Aun Weor, *The Zodiacal Course*

Lilith: (also Lilit; Hebrew, "the night visitor") An ancient symbol appearing in Sumerian mythology (4000 BC), later known in Kabbalah as the feminine half or the first "wife" of Adam. After the division of sexes, she became the source of many demonic spirits (elementaries) who plague mankind, including the sucubi and incubi generated by masturbation and sexual fantasy.

"In a hole by the great, supernal abyss, there is a certain female, a spirit above all spirits. We have explained that its name is Lilit. She was first with Adam, being his wife... In ancient books, it has been said that Lilit fled from Adam before that, namely before Eve was prepared. We did not understand it this way, because this female, Lilit, was with him. As long as this woman, Eve, was not made to be with Adam, Lilit was with him. When Eve was designed to be with him, Lilit fled to the sea, destined to harm the world." —Zohar

"...Lilith, the great mother of the demons..." —Zohar

"Lilith is the mother of abortions, homosexuality, and in general, all kinds of crimes against Nature." —Samael Aun Weor, *The Perfect Matrimony*

"Kabbalistic traditions tell us that Adam had two wives: Lilith and Nahemah. It is stated that Lilith is the mother of abortion, homosexuality, mother of sexual degeneration, and Nahemah is the mother of adultery, fornication, etc. Lilith and Nahemah are the two aspects of infrasexuality. These two women correspond to two sub-

merged spheres within the very interior of the Earth, the infradimensional and the mineral."
—Samael Aun Weor, *Tarot and Kabbalah*

Lunar: From Latin lunaris "of the moon," from luna luna, the Moon. The Romans called the moon goddess Luna, which in Greek is Selene.

In esotericism, the term lunar is generally used in concert with its solar companion, and this duality can have many implications. In Western esotericism and the writings of Samael Aun Weor, the lunar aspect is seen as feminine, cold, and polarized as negative (not "bad," just the opposite polarity of solar, which is positive). In Asian mysticism, the symbolic genders are often reversed, with the lunar current seen as masculine and related to Chandra, the masculine moon god.

Some example uses of the term lunar:

1. In general "lunar" can indicate something that proceeds mechanically, automatically, — like the movements of the Moon, tides, seasons, etc. — according to the fundamental natural laws. While this is perfectly normal, it is inferior to the solar attributes, which are not bound by mechanical movements, but instead have liberty, freedom of movement, etc.

2. In another context, for example within the body, there are lunar and solar currents. Within us, the lunar current is fallen into disgrace and must be restored, while the solar current remains intact.

3. There are solar and lunar religions: a lunar religion faces backwards, looking only at the

past, and remains attached to traditions, habits, mechanical rules. A lunar mind is similar.

4. The lunar bodies are the vehicles we receive from nature automatically: the physical body, vital body, and astral-mental body. Since they were made by nature, they must be returned to nature, thus they are not immortal, eternal, thereby illustrating the need to create solar bodies, which transcend the mechanical, lunar laws of nature.

Magic: The word magic is derived from the ancient word "mag" that means priest. Real magic is the work of a priest. A real magician is a priest.

"Magic, according to Novalis, is the art of influencing the inner world consciously." —Samael Aun Weor, *The Mystery of the Golden Blossom*

"When magic is explained as it really is, it seems to make no sense to fanatical people. They prefer to follow their world of illusions." —Samael Aun Weor, *The Revolution of Beelzebub*

Mantra: (Sanskrit, literally "mind protection") A sacred word or sound. The use of sacred words and sounds is universal throughout all religions and mystical traditions, because the root of all creation is in the Great Breath or the Word, the Logos. "In the beginning was the Word..."

Master: Like many terms related to spirituality, this one is grossly misunderstood. Although many people claim to be "masters," the truth is that the terrestrial person is only a terrestrial person. The only one who can be a master is the Innermost, Atman, the Father, Chesed.

"And, behold, one came and said unto [Jesus], Good master, what good thing shall I do, that

I may have eternal life? And he said unto him, Why callest thou me good? there is none good but one, that is, God." —Matthew 19

"The value of the human person which is the intellectual animal called human being is less than the ash of a cigarette. However, the fools feel themselves to be giants. Unfortunately, within all the pseudo-esoteric currents a great amount of mythomaniac people exist, individuals who feel themselves to be masters, people who enjoy when others call them masters, individuals who believe themselves to be Gods, individuals who presume to be saints. The only one who is truly great is the Spirit, the Innermost. We, the intellectual animals, are leaves that the wind tosses about... No student of occultism is a master. True masters are only those who have reached the Fifth Initiation of Major Mysteries [Tiphereth, the causal body]. Before the Fifth Initiation nobody is a master." —Samael Aun Weor, *The Perfect Matrimony*

"You [if you have reached levels of initiation] are not the master, you are only the sinning shadow of He who has never sinned. Remember that only your internal Lamb is the master. Remember that even though your internal God is a Hierarch of fire, you, poor slug, are only a human being and as a human being you will always be judged. Your internal Lamb could be a planetary God, but you, poor slug of the mud, do not forget, always remember that you are only the shadow of your God. Poor sinning shadow..! Do not say "I am this God" or "I am that master," because you are only a shadow that must resolve to die and be slaughtered in order not to serve as an obstacle for your internal God. It is necessary for you to reach supreme humbleness." —Samael Aun Weor, *The Aquarian Message*

"Do not accept external masters in the physical plane. Learn how to travel in the astral body, and when you are skillful in the astral, choose an authentic master of Major Mysteries of the White Brotherhood and consecrate unto him the most absolute devotion and the most profound respect." —Samael Aun Weor, *The Zodiacal Course*

Meditation: "When the esotericist submerges himself into meditation, what he seeks is information." —Samael Aun Weor

"It is urgent to know how to meditate in order to comprehend any psychic aggregate, or in other words, any psychological defect. It is indispensable to know how to work with all our heart and with all our soul, if we want the elimination to occur." —Samael Aun Weor, *The Gnostic Bible: The Pistis Sophia Unveiled*

"1. The Gnostic must first attain the ability to stop the course of his thoughts, the capacity to not think. Indeed, only the one who achieves that capacity will hear the Voice of the Silence.

"2. When the Gnostic disciple attains the capacity to not think, then he must learn to concentrate his thoughts on only one thing.

"3. The third step is correct meditation. This brings the first flashes of the new consciousness into the mind.

"4. The fourth step is contemplation, ecstasy or Samadhi. This is the state of Turiya (perfect clairvoyance)." —Samael Aun Weor, *The Perfect Matrimony*

Ninth Sphere: In Kabbalah, a reference to the sephirah Yesod of the Tree of Life (Kabbalah). When you place the Tree of Life over your body, you see that Yesod is related to your sexual organs.

"The Ninth Sphere of the Kabbalah is sex." —Samael Aun Weor, *The Perfect Matrimony*

The Ninth Sphere also refers to the sephirah Yesod and to the lowest sphere of the Klipoth.

"The great Master Hilarion IX said that in ancient times, to descend into the Ninth Sphere was the maximum ordeal for the supreme dignity of the Hierophant. Hermes, Buddha, Jesus Christ, Dante, Zoroaster, Mohammed, Rama, Krishna, Pythagoras, Plato and many others, had to descend into the Ninth Sphere in order to work with the fire and the water which is the origin of worlds, beasts, human beings and Gods. Every authentic white initiation begins here." —Samael Aun Weor, *The Aquarian Message*

Objective: [See: Subjective]

Ray of Creation: The light of the Ain Soph Aur, also known as the Okidanokh, Quetzalcoatl, Kulkulcan, Krestos, and Christ. This Ray decends as a lightning bolt, creating and illuminating all the levels of existence.

"The proper arrangement of the Ray of Creation is as follows:

　1. Absolute - Protocosmos

　2. All the worlds from all of the clusters of galaxies - Ayocosmos

3. A galaxy or group of suns - Macrocosmos

4. The sun, solar system - Deuterocosmos

5. The Earth, or any of the planets - Mesocosmos

6. The Philosophical Earth, Human Being - Microcosmos

7. The Abyss, Hell - Tritocosmos

"The brothers and sisters of the Gnostic Movement must deeply comprehend the esoteric knowledge which we give in this Christmas Message, in order for them to exactly know the place that they occupy in the Ray of Creation." — Samael Aun Weor, *The Elimination of Satan's Tail*

Return: The process of the soul entering into a new born physical body as determined by karma and circumstance, rather than "by choice" as is popularly imagined. Returning into a physical body as determined by cause and effect (karmic debt) is the norm for all humanoid creatures on this planet, and a mechanical process, not a conscious choice, in spite of popular belief.

"Millions of people speak about the laws of reincarnation and karma, without having directly experienced their deep significance. Really, the lunar ego returns, re-embodies, penetrates into a new womb, but that cannot be called reincarnation; speaking with precision, we will say that that is "return." Reincarnation is something else; reincarnation is only for masters, for sacred individuals, for the Twice-born, for those who already possess the Being. The lunar ego returns and, according to the law of recurrence, it repeats in each life the same actions, the same dramas of preceding lives. The spiral line is the line of life and each life is either repeated in a more elevated, evolving spiral, or in a lower, devolving spiral. Each life is a repetition of the past one, plus its good or bad, pleasant or unpleasant, consequences. In a resolved and definitive manner, many people descend from life to life on the devolving spiral line, until finally entering the infernal worlds. The one who wants to attain in-depth Self-realization must liberate himself from the vicious circle of the evolving and devolving laws of nature." —Samael Aun Weor, *Practical Astrology*

Samadhi: (Sanskrit) Literally means "union" or "combination" and its Tibetan equivilent means "adhering to that which is profound and defini-tive," or ting nge dzin, meaning "To hold unwav-eringly, so there is no movement." Related terms include satori, ecstasy, manteia, etc. Samadhi is a state of consciousness. In the west, the term is used to describe an ecstatic state of conscious-ness in which the Essence escapes the painful limitations of the mind (the "I") and therefore experiences what is real: the Being, the Great Reality. There are many levels of Samadhi. In the sutras and tantras the term Samadhi has a much broader application whose precise interpretation depends upon which school and teaching is us-ing it.

"Ecstasy is not a nebulous state, but a transcen-dental state of wonderment, which is associated with perfect mental clarity." —Samael Aun Weor, *The Elimination of Satan's Tail*

Second Death: A mechanical process in nature experienced by those souls who within the allotted time fail to reach union with their inner divinity (i.e. known as self-realization, liberation, religare, yoga, moksha, etc). The Second Death is the complete dissolution of the ego (karma, defects, sins) in the infernal regions of nature, which after unimaginable quantities of suffering, proportional to the density of the psyche, in the end purifies the Essence (consciousness) so that it may try again to perfect itself and reach the union with the Being.

"He that overcometh (the sexual passion) shall inherit all things; and I will be his God (I will incarnate myself within him), and he shall be my son (because he is a Christified one), But the fearful (the tenebrous, cowards, unbelievers), and unbelieving, and the abominable, and murderers, and whoremongers, and sorcerers, and idolaters, and all liars, shall have their part in the lake which burneth with fire and brimstone: which is the second death. (Revelation 21) This lake which burns with fire and brimstone is the lake of carnal passion. This lake is related with the lower animal depths of the human being and its atomic region is the abyss. The tenebrous slowly disintegrate themselves within the abyss until they die. This is the second death." —Samael Aun Weor, *The Aquarian Message*

"When the bridge called "Antakarana," which communicates the divine triad with its "inferior essence", is broken, the inferior essence (trapped into the ego) is left separated and is sunk into the abyss of destructive forces, where it (its ego) disintegrates little by little. This is the Second Death of which the Apocalypse speaks; this is the state of consciousness called "Avitchi." — Samael Aun Weor, *The Zodiacal Course*

" The Second Death is really painful. The ego feels as if it has been divided in different parts, the fingers fall off, its arms, its legs. It suffers through a tremendous breakdown." —Samael Aun Weor, from the lecture *The Mysteries of Life and Death*

Self-observation: An exercise of attention, in which one learns to become an indifferent observer of one's own psychological process. True Self-observation is an active work of directed attention, without the interference of thought.

"We need attention intentionally directed towards the interior of our own selves. This is not a passive attention. Indeed, dynamic attention proceeds from the side of the observer, while thoughts and emotions belong to the side which is observed." —Samael Aun Weor, *Treatise of Revolutionary Psychology*

Self-realization: The achievement of perfect knowledge. This phrase is better stated as, "The realization of the Innermost Self," or "The realization of the true nature of self." At the ultimate level, this is the experiential, conscious knowledge of the Absolute, which is synonymous with Emptiness, Shunyata, or Non-being.

Self-remembering: A state of active consciousness, controlled by will, that begins with awareness of being here and now. This state has many levels (see: Consciousness). True Self-remembering occurs without thought or mental processing: it is a state of conscious perception and includes the remembrance or awareness of the inner Being.

"Even though it seems incredible, when aspirants are observing themselves they do not remember their Self. Indeed, beyond any doubt, aspirants do not perceive their Self; they have no cognizance of their Self. It seems inconceivable that when Gnostic aspirants self-observe their mannerisms when they laugh, speak, walk, etc., they forget their Self; this is incredible, but true. Nevertheless, it is indispensable to exert the remembrance of our Self while we are observing ourselves. This is fundamental in order to attain the awakening of the consciousness. Self-observing, self-knowing, without forgetting our Self, is terribly difficult, but frightfully urgent in order to attain the awakening of the consciousness. What we are stating seems trivial to the people who ignore that they are asleep; they ignore that they do not remember their Self, not even when they look at their bodies in a full-length mirror, moreover, not even when they observe themselves in detail meticulously. The forgetfulness of our Self, the lack of remembering of our Self, is indeed the causa causorum of all human ignorance." —Samael Aun Weor, *Light from Darkness*

"Behold how difficult is to remain with the consciousness awake from instant to instant, from moment to moment, from second after second; however, if one has true longings for becoming fully awakened - this is the beginning - one must not forget oneself, not even for a moment. Yes, one must keep remembering oneself wherever one walks - in any living room, or whichever street one goes around by walking, jogging or riding a car, whether it be at night or at daylight; wherever one might be, at work or in the shop, anywhere, one must remember oneself while in the presence of any beautiful object, or while before any window-shop where very beautiful things are being shown, etc., in other words, one must not become identified with anything that one likes or is captivated with." —Samael Aun Weor, The Key of SOL

Semen: In the esoteric tradition of pure sexuality, the word semen refers to the sexual energy of the organism, whether male or female. This is because male and female both carry the "seed" within: in order to create, the two "seeds" must be combined. In common usage: "The smaller, usually motile male reproductive cell of most organisms that reproduce sexually." English semen originally meant 'seed of male animals' in the 14th century, and it was not applied to human males until the 18th century. It came from Latin semen, 'seed of plants,' from serere, 'to sow.' The Latin goes back to the Indo-European root *se-, source of seed, disseminate, season, seminar, and seminal. The word seminary (used for religious schools) is derived from semen and originally meant 'seedbed.' That the semen is the source of all virtue is known from the word "seminal," derived from the Latin "semen," and which is defined as "highly original and influencing the development of future events: a seminal artist; seminal ideas."

"According to Yogic science, semen exists in a subtle form throughout the whole body. It is found in a subtle state in all the cells of the body. It is withdrawn and elaborated into a gross form in the sexual organ under the influence of the sexual will and sexual excitement. An Oordhvareta Yogi (one who has stored up the seminal energy in the brain after sublimating the same into spiritual energy) not only converts the semen into Ojas, but checks through his Yogic power, through purity in thought, word and deed, the very formation of semen by the secretory cells or testes or seeds. This is a great secret." —Sri Swami Sivananda, *Brahmacharya* (Celibacy)

Sexual Magic: The word magic is derived from the ancient word magos "one of the members of the learned and priestly class," from O.Pers. magush, possibly from PIE *magh- "to be able, to have power." [Quoted from Online Etymology Dictionary].

"All of us possess some electrical and magnetic forces within, and, just like a magnet, we exert a force of attraction and repulsion... Between lovers that magnetic force is particularly powerful and its action has a far-reaching effect." —Samael Aun Weor, *The Mystery of the Golden Blossom*

Sexual magic refers to an ancient science that has been known and protected by the purest, most spiritually advanced human beings, whose purpose and goal is the harnessing and perfection of our sexual forces. A more accurate translation of sexual magic would be "sexual priesthood." In ancient times, the priest was always accompanied by a priestess, for they represent the divine forces at the base of all creation: the masculine and feminine, the Yab-Yum, Ying-Yang, Father-Mother: the Elohim. Unfortunately, the term "sexual magic" has been grossly misinterpreted by mistaken persons such as Aleister Crowley, who advocated a host of degenerated practices, all of which belong solely to the lowest and most perverse mentality and lead only to the enslavement of the consciousness, the worship of lust and desire, and the decay of humanity. True, upright, heavenly sexual magic is the natural harnessing of our latent forces, making them active and harmonious with nature and the divine, and which leads to the perfection of the human being.

"People are filled with horror when they hear about sexual magic; however, they are not filled with horror when they give themselves to all kinds of sexual perversion and to all kinds of carnal passion." —Samael Aun Weor, *The Perfect Matrimony*

Sephirah: (or sefira; Hebrew) plural: sephiroth. Literally means "counting" or "enumeration", yet given the flexibility of Hebrew has other roots, such as sefer (text), sippur (recounting a story), sappir (sapphire, brilliance, luminary), separ (boundary), and safra (scribe).

A sephirah is a symbol used in Kabbalah to represent levels of manifestation ranging from the very subtle to the very dense, and which apply to everything that exists, from the grandest scale to the most minute. Generally, these levels are represented in a structure of ten sephiroth called "the Tree of Life." This ten-sphered structure is a simplified arrangement of more complex renderings.

1. An emanation of Deity.

"The ten sephiroth of universal vibration emerge from the Ain Soph, which is the microcosmic star that guides our interior. This star is the real Being of our Being. Ten sephiroth are spoken of, but in reality there are twelve; the Ain Soph is the eleventh, and its tenebrous antithesis is in the abyss, which is the twelfth sephirah. These are twelve spheres or universal regions that interpenetrate each other without confusion." —Samael Aun Weor, *Tarot and Kabbalah*

1. Kether: The Father

2. Chokmah: The Son

3. Binah: The Holy Spirit

4. Chesed: Atman, the Innermost, our Divine Being

5. Geburah: The feminine Spiritual Soul, Buddhi

6. Tiphereth: Superior Manas, the Human Soul

7. Netzach: The Solar Mind, the Christ Mind

8. Hod: The legitimate astral solar body

9. Yesod: The Cubic Stone, sex

10. Malkuth: The physical body

"The sephiroth are atomic. The ten sephiroth can be reduced into three tables:

1. A quantum table of the radiant energy that comes from the sun

2. An atomic weight table of the elements of nature

3. A molecular weight table of compounds

"This is Jacob's ladder, which goes from Earth to heaven. All of the worlds of cosmic consciousness are reduced to the three tables." —Samael Aun Weor, *Tarot and Kabbalah*

"A sephirah cannot be understood only in one plane, because it is of a quadruple nature. Therefore, the Kabbalists clearly express the fact that there are four worlds." —Samael Aun Weor, *Tarot and Kabbalah*

2. A name of the Divine Mother.

"The ten known sephiroth come from Sephirah, the Divine Mother, who resides in the heart temple. The mantra of the Divine Mother is IO which is the 10 emanations of Prakriti, in other words, the 10 (ten) sephiroth." —Samael Aun Weor, *Tarot and Kabbalah*

Solar Bodies: A reference to the sacred vehicle(s) that the initiate must construct in order to ascend into the superior worlds. Various traditions number them differently depending upon the point of view. The physical, vital, astral, mental, and causal bodies that are created through the beginning stages of Alchemy/Tantra and that provide a basis for existence in their corresponding levels of nature, just as the physical body does in the physical world. These bodies or vehicles are superior due to being created out of Solar (Christic) Energy, as opposed to the inferior, lunar bodies we receive from nature. Also known as the Wedding Garment (Christianity), the Merkabah (Kabbalah), To Soma Heliakon (Greek), and Sahu (Egyptian).

"All the Masters of the White Lodge, the Angels, Archangels, Thrones, Seraphim, Virtues, etc., etc.,

etc. are garbed with the Solar Bodies. Only those who have Solar Bodies have the Being incarnated. Only someone who possesses the Being is an authentic Human Being." —Samael Aun Weor, *The Esoteric Treatise of Hermetic Astrology*

"All flesh [is] not the same flesh: but [there is] one [kind of] flesh of men, another flesh of beasts, another of fishes, [and] another of birds. [There are] also celestial bodies, and bodies terrestrial: but the glory of the celestial [is] one, and the [glory] of the terrestrial [is] another. [There is] one glory of the sun, and another glory of the moon, and another glory of the stars: for [one] star differeth from [another] star in glory." — Paul, from 1 Corinthians 15

Subjective: "What do modern psychologists understand as 'objective?' They understand it to be that which is external to the mind: the physical, the tangible, the material.

"Yet, they are totally mistaken, because when analysing the term "subjective," we see that it signifies "sub, under," that which is below the range of our perceptions. What is below our perceptions? Is it not perhaps the Infernal Worlds? Is it not perhaps subjective that which is in the physical or beneath the physical? So, what is truly subjective is what is below the limits of our perceptions.

"Psychologists do not know how to use the former terms correctly.

"Objective: the light, the resplendence; it is that which contains the Truth, clarity, lucidity.

"Subjective: the darkness, the tenebrous. The subjective elements of perception are the outcome of seeing, hearing, touching, smelling and tasting. All of these are perceptions of what we see in the third dimension. For example, in one cube we see only length, width and height. We do not see the fourth dimension because we are bottled up within the ego. The subjective elements of perception are constituted by the ego with all of its "I's." —Samael Aun Weor, *Tarot and Kabbalah*

Tantra: Sanskrit for "continuum" or "unbroken stream." from Sanskrit tantram, lit. "loom, warp," hence "groundwork, system, doctrine," from tan "to stretch, extend." Tantra refers first (1) to the continuum of vital energy that sustains all existence, and second (2) to the class of knowledge and practices that harnesses that vital energy, thereby transforming the practitioner. There are many schools of Tantra, but they can be classified in three types: White, Grey and Black, according to their purity; White demands ethical purity, while Black encourages lust, pride, etc. Tantra has long been known in the West as Alchemy. In Asian religions, there is a corresponding class of books called Tantras.

"In the view of Tantra, the body's vital energies are the vehicles of the mind. When the vital energies are pure and subtle, one's state of mind will be accordingly affected. By transforming these bodily energies we transform the state of consciousness." —The 14th Dalai Lama

Vulcan: The Latin or Roman name for the Greek god Hephaestus, known by the Egyptians as Ptah. A god of fire with a deep and ancient mythology, commonly remembered as the blacksmith who forges weapons for gods and heroes. Vulcan is very important in the tradition of Alchemy. In Hinduism, he is symbolized by Tvastri, later called Visvakarma.

"To Hephaistos (Hephaestus), Fumigation from Frankincense and Manna. Strong, mighty Hephaistos, bearing splendid light, unwearied fire, with flaming torrents bright: strong-handed, deathless, and of art divine, pure element, a portion of the world is thine: all-taming artist, all-diffusive power, 'tis thine, supreme, all substance to devour: aither, sun, moon, and stars, light pure and clear, for these thy lucid parts [of fire] to men appear. To thee all dwellings, cities, tribes belong, diffused through mortal bodies, rich and strong. Hear, blessed power, to holy rites incline, and all propitious on the incense shine: suppress the rage of fire's unwearied frame, and still preserve our nature's vital flame." —Orphic Hymn

"All of the processes related with sexual transmutation are possible because of the intervention of the Vital Body. This is the Archaeous that elaborates the blood and the semen in the human organism. This is Vulcan that transmutes the seminal liquor into Christic Energy. The Vital Body is the vehicle of the Soul-Consciousness in the human being. The consciousness is the flame and the vital body is the wick. Vulcan exists within the Microcosmos and within the Macrocosmos, in the human being and in Nature. The great Vulcan of Nature is Eden, the Ethereal Plane." —Samael Aun Weor, *Alchemy and Kabbalah in the Tarot*

Quotes from Paracelsus:

"The office of Vulcan is the separation of the good from the bad. So the Art of Vulcan, which is Alchemy, is like unto death, by which the eternal and the temporal are divided one from another. So also this art might be called the death of things." —De Morbis Metallicis, Lib. I., Tract III., c. 1.

"Vulcan is an astral and not a corporal fabricator." —De Caduco Matricis, Par. VI.

"The artist working in metals and other minerals transforms them into other colours, and in so doing his operation is like that of the heaven itself. For as the artist excocts by means of Vulcan, or the igneous element, so heaven performs the work of coction through the Sun. The Sun, therefore, is the Vulcan of heaven accomplishing coction in the earth." —De Icteritiis.

"Vulcan is the fabricator and architect of all things, nor is his habitation in heaven only, that is, in the firmament, but equally in all the other elements." —Lib. Meteorum, c. 4.

"Where the three prime principles are wanting, there also the igneous essence is absent. The Igneous Vulcan is nothing else but sulfur, Sal Nitrum, and Mercury." —Ibid., c.5.

White Brotherhood or Lodge: That ancient collection of pure souls who maintain the highest and most sacred of sciences: White Magic or White Tantra. It is called White due to its purity and cleanliness. This "Brotherhood" or "Lodge" includes human beings of the highest order from every race, culture, creed and religion, and of both sexes.

Yoga: (Sanskrit) "union." Similar to the Latin "religare," the root of the word "religion." In Tibetan, it is "rnal-'byor" which means "union with the fundamental nature of reality."

"The word YOGA comes from the root Yuj which means to join, and in its spiritual sense, it is that process by which the human spirit is brought into near and conscious communion with, or is merged in, the Divine Spirit, according as the nature of the human spirit is held to be separate from (Dvaita, Visishtadvaita) or one with (Advaita) the Divine Spirit." —Swami Sivananda, *Kundalini Yoga*

"Patanjali defines Yoga as the suspension of all the functions of the mind. As such, any book on Yoga, which does not deal with these three aspects of the subject, viz., mind, its functions and the method of suspending them, can he safely laid aside as unreliable and incomplete." —Swami Sivananda, *Practical Lessons In Yoga*

"The word yoga means in general to join one's mind with an actual fact..." —The 14th Dalai Lama

"The soul aspires for the union with his Innermost, and the Innermost aspires for the union with his Glorian." —Samael Aun Weor, *The Revolution of Beelzebub*

"All of the seven schools of Yoga are within Gnosis, yet they are in a synthesized and absolutely practical way. There is Tantric Hatha Yoga in the practices of the Maithuna (Sexual Magic). There is practical Raja Yoga in the work with the chakras. There is Gnana / Jnana Yoga in our practices and mental disciplines which we have cultivated in secrecy for millions of years. We have Bhakti Yoga in our prayers and Rituals. We have Laya Yoga in our meditation and respiratory exercises. Samadhi exists in our practices with the Maithuna and during our deep meditations. We live the path of Karma Yoga in our upright actions, in our upright thoughts, in our upright feelings, etc." —Samael Aun Weor, *The Revolution of Beelzebub*

"Yoga does not consist in sitting cross-legged for six hours or stopping the beatings of the heart or getting oneself buried underneath the ground for a week or a month. These are all physical feats only. Yoga is the science that teaches you the method of uniting the individual will with the Cosmic Will. Yoga transmutes the unregenerate nature and increases energy, vitality, vigour, and bestows longevity and a high standard of health." —Swami Sivananda, *Autobiography*

"Brahmacharya [chastity] is the very foundation of Yoga." —Swami Sivananda

"The Yoga that we require today is actually ancient Gnostic Christian Yoga, which absolutely rejects the idea of Hatha Yoga. We do not recommend Hatha Yoga simply because, spiritually speaking, the acrobatics of this discipline are fruitless; they should be left to the acrobats of the circus." —Samael Aun Weor, *The Yellow Book*

"Yoga has been taught very badly in the Western world. Multitudes of pseudo-sapient Yogis have spread the false belief that the true Yogi must be an infrasexual (an enemy of sex). Some of these false yogis have never even visited India; they are infrasexual pseudo-yogis. These ignoramuses believe that they are going to achieve in-depth realization only with the yogic exercises, such as asanas, pranayamas, etc. Not only do they have such false beliefs, but what is worse is that they propagate them; thus, they misguide many people away from the difficult, straight, and narrow door that leads unto the light. No authentically initiated Yogi from India would ever think that he could achieve his inner self-realization with pranayamas or asanas, etc. Any legitimate Yogi from India knows very well that such yogic exercises are only co-assistants that are very useful for their health and for the development of their powers, etc. Only the Westerners and pseudo-yogis have within their minds the belief that they can achieve Self-realization with such exercises. Sexual Magic is practiced very secretly within the Ashrams of India. Any true yogi initiate from India works with the Arcanum A.Z.F. This is taught by the great Yogis from India that have visited the Western world, and if it has not been taught by these great, initiated Hindustani Yogis, if it has not been published in their books of Yoga, it was in order to avoid scandals. You can be absolutely sure that the Yogis who do not practice Sexual Magic will never achieve birth in the superior worlds. Thus, whosoever affirms the contrary is a liar, an impostor." —Samael Aun Weor, *Alchemy and Kabbalah in the Tarot*

Yogi: (Sanskrit) male yoga practitioner.

Yogini: (Sanskrit) female yoga practitioner.

Index

Index

About the Author

His name is Hebrew סמאל אונ ואור, and is pronounced "sam-ayel on vay-or." You may not have heard of him, but Samael Aun Weor changed the world.

In 1950, in his first two books, he became the first person to reveal the esoteric secret hidden in all the world's great religions, and for that, accused of "healing the ill," he was put in prison. Nevertheless, he did not stop. Between 1950 and 1977 – merely twenty-seven years – not only did Samael Aun Weor write over sixty books on the most difficult subjects in the world, such as consciousness, kabbalah, physics, tantra, meditation, etc., in which he deftly exposed the singular root of all knowledge — which he called Gnosis — he simultaneously inspired millions of people across the entire span of Latin America: stretching across twenty countries and an area of more than 21,000,000 kilometers, founding schools everywhere, even in places without electricity or post offices.

During those twenty-seven years, he experienced all the extremes that humanity could give him, from adoration to death threats, and in spite of the enormous popularity of his books and lectures, he renounced an income, refused recognitions, walked away from accolades, and consistently turned away those who would worship him. He held as friends both presidents and peasants, and yet remained a mystery to all.

When one reflects on the effort and will it requires to perform even day to day tasks, it is astonishing to consider the herculean efforts required to accomplish what he did in such a short time. But, there is a reason: he was a man who knew who he was, and what he had to do. A true example of compassion and selfless service, Samael Aun Weor dedicated the whole of his life to freely helping anyone and everyone find the path out of suffering. His mission was to show all of humanity the universal source of all spiritual traditions, which he did not only through his writings and lectures, but also through his actions.

Your book reviews matter.

Glorian Publishing is a very small non-profit organization, thus we have no money to spend on marketing and advertising. Fortunately, there is a proven way to gain the attention of readers: book reviews. Mainstream book reviewers won't review these books, but you can.

The path of liberation requires the daily balance of three active factors:

- · birth of virtue
- · death of vice
- · sacrifice for others

Writing book reviews is a powerful way to sacrifice for others. By writing book reviews on popular websites, you help to make the books more visible to humanity, and you might help save a soul from suffering. Will you do your part to help us show these wonderful teachings to others? Take a moment today to write a review.

Donate

Glorian Publishing is a non-profit publisher dedicated to spreading the sacred universal doctrine to suffering humanity. All of our works are made possible by the kindness and generosity of sponsors. If you would like to make a tax-deductible donation, you may send it to the address below, or visit our website for other alternatives. If you would like to sponsor the publication of a book, please contact us at (844) 945-6742 or help@glorian.org.

Glorian Publishing
PO Box 209
Clinton, CT 06413 US
Phone: (844) 945-6742

VISIT US ONLINE AT glorian.org